Paddling the Northern Forest Canoe Trail:

A Journey Through New England History

By Sam Brakeley

The Northern Forest Canoe Trail

A 740 mile paddling trail that runs from Old Forge, NY to Fort Kent, ME

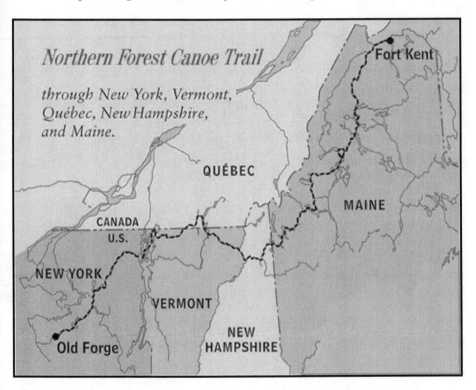

Introduction

Perhaps a week before we left to begin our journey on the Northern Forest Canoe Trail, I was driving in the car with my father. We were chatting about this and that when suddenly he asked me, "Why? Why this trail?" I don't recall my exact answer, although it was probably something along the lines of 'Why not?' or 'Because it's there,' some typical flip response that perhaps Sir Edmund Hillary or Amundsen used to answer similar questions. I quickly realized, however, that these words were inadequate and I thought it over with a little more care that night. Why *was* I doing this trip? Why this trail, and not some other? And why was I doing another wilderness trip at all, instead of some other endeavor? (Like an internship, my father would doubtless point out, to further your résumé and future.) My answer now, is as follows.

To put it simply, I love the woods. I love the outdoors, the wilderness, the plants, animals, and nature. I love the feel of sun, rain, hot, cold, whatever, on my face, and only out 'there' do I feel utterly at peace. I love that feeling of complete freedom from all else, with the only thoughts running through your mind of what's around the bend, or what's cooking for dinner tonight. I love the simplicity of traveling slowly every day, free from turnpikes and railways, and instead cruising silently through the forest. I love the basic challenges of a tough portage, a tough whitewater set, building a fire in the rain, or paddling into heavy headwinds. Watching a moose forage for dinner, an eagle soar on the thermals, the rain drip, drip, drip from the branches, or the fire flit in and out of sticks of wood, hungrily devouring fuel as I hungrily wait for the water to boil, all combine to bring me a sense of inner peace achievable in no other setting. That is why I return again and again to the woods, and why I will continue to do so until I am so old and infirm that I can only dream. I can't help it. It's part of my DNA. I'd argue it's part of everyone's DNA, but that will come later.

It certainly is a way of escaping the hullabaloo and restless pace of 'real life'. As my college career neared completion I looked with trepidation on the coming years. Could I flout tradition, respectability and civilization's norms, and remain true to myself by embracing a life in the woods, or would the world's responsibilities drag me down and hold me hostage? I don't ever want to live a life that does not involve the wilderness. I don't ever want to leave the forests or lakes, or travel without a paddle in my hand or hiking boots on my feet. Sigurd F. Olson, a Minnesota conservationist and paddler, described canoe journeys better than I ever could in *The Singing Wilderness.*

> The movement of a canoe is like a reed in the wind. Silence
> is part of it, and the sounds of lapping water, bird songs, and
> wind in the trees. It is part of the medium through which it
> floats, the sky, the water, the shores... There is a magic in the

feel of a paddle and the movement of a canoe, a magic compounded of distance, adventure, solitude, and peace. The way of a canoe is the way of the wilderness, and of a freedom almost forgotten. It is an antidote to insecurity, the open door to waterways of ages past and a way of life with profound and abiding satisfactions. When a man is part of his canoe, he is part of all that canoes have ever known.

But why this trip? Why this particular trail? I was born and bred in New England, and while I have traveled extensively and seen New England from the mountain ridges and peaks, I had never taken a river trip here. My previous experience has been in the waters of Canada, and the official ribbon-cutting of the Northern Forest Canoe Trail in 2006 opened this new door for me. It was clearly a challenge, with significant whitewater, long portages, and tough upstream sections. It traverses some of the wilder regions of New England, many of which I'd never been to before. And finally it was a new trail. Not many more than a handful of people had thru-paddled it and the idea of being a member of that select few certainly appealed to me.

A trip through the wilderness, whether it is one day, one week, one month, or longer, should be taken by all as part of a soul-searching journey. I truly believe that many of the world's ills can be traced to a lack of wilderness, a lack of escape, and a lack of a place to settle oneself, to re-center, and to begin again, rested and rejuvenated from time spent out of doors. After long periods of time 'away', I am able to re-focus, and to re-apply myself to the business of living. But without these periods of re-charging, I would be a lost soul indeed.

My own particular journey occurred at a singular time in my life. I would be a senior in college in the coming fall, and one short year after my paddle first tasted water on the NFCT, I would be on my own. This journey, then, was not only one last hurrah before I faced the truly adult world but also a voyage of self. What exactly was I going to do with my life, and how can I continue to spend time between the gunwales of a canoe?

I still continue to struggle with some of these questions, but enough of that for now. So let the following pages motivate and entertain you, then go find a map, and dream of the possibilities. The world is a big place, and there is a bend just waiting for you to go find what's hiding on the other side.

Chapter 1: Starting Out

Sophomore year of college I was talking with my good friend Andy, and told him of a new canoe trail I just heard about.

"I was out paddling on the Saranac Lakes, and saw a small yellow sign for something called the Northern Forest Canoe Trail. I looked it up and it runs all the way from New York to Maine, and looks pretty fantastic."

A big grin lit Andy's face, "Yeah I just read about that too! It's brand new and only a couple people have done it. You want to?"

And that is pretty much how it started. As described above I am a passionate outdoorsman, and Andy had significant experience working as a staffman at a canoe camp in Maine. We knew each other well at school playing rugby together and knew we enjoyed each other's company. Andy is very easygoing and extremely friendly. He seems to have a nearly perpetual grin and little rubs him the wrong way. I knew I could easily endure his company for six weeks. The only question would be could he endure mine. He too was passionate about the outdoors. We vowed to take the next chance and set out on the expedition. The summer of 2008 we were both busy – Andy working and I hiking – but we made tentative plans for the summer of 2009. As it grew closer we both committed, and before we knew it we were packing gear and creating an itinerary. We were going to paddle the Northern Forest Canoe Trail.

The Northern Forest Canoe Trail, a canoe and kayak trail, opened officially in 2006. As described by the Northern Forest Canoe Trail organization,

> The Northern Forest Canoe Trail is a long-distance
> paddling trail connecting the major watersheds across the
> Adirondacks and Northern New England. In the 740-mile
> traverse across New York, Vermont, Quebec, New
> Hampshire, and Maine, the Trail links communities and
> wild places, offering canoeists and kayakers a lifetime
> of paddling destinations and adventures.

It traverses rivers, lakes and streams along traditional water routes used by Native Americans, and later European explorers, fur trappers and colonists. We planned on it taking about six weeks. Our chosen craft was the canoe, which has such a distinguished history that I'm sure the reader will permit me to explore it a little before entering the narrative of our journey.

Native Americans used canoes almost exclusively for water travel in much of the contiguous United States. Multiple variations have been employed elsewhere (kayaks and umiaks further north and dugouts further south and west), but the traditional bark canoe is perfectly suited to river and lake travel in New England. Its light frame and quick maneuverability are admirably designed for the stony rapids, quick currents, and occasionally long portages encountered during a journey through the North American hinterland. They were constructed to varied lengths, up to nearly fifty feet in some cases, but most were from 14-20 feet in length. Used for transportation, hunting, traveling and even war, they were an essential part of most Native American culture.

Europeans initially scoffed at the canoe's small size and light weight. They viewed their larger seafaring ships with pride and looked with condescension upon the small crafts they found in the New World. This opinion quickly changed, however, once they attempted to voyage inland. Rivers are natural highways through the thick New England woods, and it is a testament to the canoe's design that Europeans could make no improvements upon the original model. They were soon adopted as the mainstay of the burgeoning fur trade throughout North America by French voyageurs, and were seen on almost all navigable rivers as the often romanticized mountain men, fur trappers, and voyageurs searched for beaver and other furbearer pelts. Much of North America was explored in this fashion, and soon few corners of the continent remained untouched by the white man.

Trading posts and forts sprang up, causing much conflict between the natives and the new-comers. Samuel de Champlain met with one of the earliest recorded canoe conflicts when he engaged a band of Iroquois on the warpath. Later, Benedict Arnold conducted the first amphibious assault in U.S. history with canoes when he attacked the British entrenched in Montreal during the Revolutionary War.

Canoes remain a prominent symbol of many of the native tribes, as well as the preferred method of water travel by many recreationists. Today they are used for pleasure, whether for an afternoon on a lake or a long journey, as well as professionally in many races throughout the world. Their construction materials have diversified to include fiberglass and aluminum, but the birch bark canoe remains an enduring tribute to the virgin North American wilderness as it was before Europeans arrived.(Poling Sr. 2000)

With such a distinguished history, it was tough not to feel at least slightly insignificant as we laid out plans for the trip. However, we both had experience with canoes, and we felt we were up to the task of handling the journey. We spent many hours planning food, gear, and itinerary, and sometimes it felt as though we would never launch. Eventually, however, we drove out to Old Forge, New York, and zero hour arrived. It was time to launch on the most ambitious canoe trip of my young life.

June 5th, Day 1 – Old Forge, New York to Seventh Lake: Several hours before I needed to, I woke up. I wasn't meeting Andy until 10:30 at the boat launch, and it was only 7:30. I tried to roll over, but the heat of the day had already entered the room, and I knew I would never be able to return to sleep. On my back, spread-eagled in an attempt to remain cool, I reflected on the coming trip. Questions like 'Will we make it?' and 'What if…?' flew through my head, along with the all-important 'What did I forget?' but I drove them from my mind. Hopefully, all was remembered during the last week of packing and planning, and if not, we'll find a replacement or manage without. Instead I tried to focus on the dawning day. Day One. One day at a time. Butterflies plagued my stomach and I was nearly consumed with doubt, self-questioning and the rhetorical "Why am I doing this again?". It disappeared with the first paddle stroke, but I couldn't help having misgivings before the start.

Knowing all this worrying was doing me little good, I got up, silently put on a pair of pants and stepped outside my motel room to see how the morning was shaping up. It promised to be a beautiful day, and I sat in the plastic chair at my doormat, looking out over the gravel parking lot onto Main Street. No more plastic chairs or motel doormats for a while, thankfully. Few cars were driving by, and no one else appeared to be awake at the motel. My last morning in civilization. My stomach rumbled at the thought of it. The last day I would be able to be completely full for a while too, since it is nearly impossible to account for the vast number of calories burned during a canoe trip.

I sat like that for an hour, absorbing the warm sunshine and letting the slight breeze play over my face, before re-entering my room, waking my girlfriend, Elizabeth, and putting a shirt on to go to breakfast. Elizabeth had graciously agreed to drive me to Old Forge, and still more graciously not gotten too angry with me for leaving her for the summer. But she understood my need to escape civilization, at least on some level, and knew it was something I needed to do. An oil change for my soul, of sorts.

We ate at a local breakfast spot where my simple question, "How big is Old Forge?" resulted in an all-employee conference on the subject. The verdict was, "about 2,000 people year-round, but it triples - *At least that, maybe even five times as much, you know,* was interjected from across the room – every summer." Much larger than I thought it would be. I feasted on French Toast, eggs, sausage, hash browns and coffee while reading about Old Forge and the surrounding area on the back of my NFCT map. The maps provided by the NFCT were fantastic. Not only were they comprehensive and (almost) 100% accurate, but the reverse side of every map was filled with descriptions of local history, lore, legends, and people. As we traveled along the Trail we were able to read up on much of the history surrounding us.

This was an integral part of the enjoyment of this trip for us. If we had wanted pure wilderness, then we would have headed further north to the wilds of Quebec. Instead, we were traveling through developed, settled New England, not a wilderness in its own right, but indeed a place filled with the ghosts of past inhabitants and wayfarers. Every inch of the Trail is covered with Native American and European history and to learn about loggers, trappers, bootleggers, paddlers, settlers, and some of the more iconic individuals who have lived on and near the NFCT was a magical opportunity for me. To not only read about them but to be able to imagine them rising from the land around me as I paddled by was a truly tangible style of learning and it made this experience a valuable one on many levels.

The town of Old Forge marks the beginning of the Northern Forest Canoe Trail and is one of the largest towns in the Adirondack Park. It began as an iron ore forge near the turn of the nineteenth century, but few settlers endured for long in the face of rocky soil, wolf predation, and cold winters. As technology improved, access increased and in 1892 a railroad was built to the area. Adirondack Park was created in the same year and it remains the largest park in the contiguous United States. Logging and tourism soon brought steady revenue to the region and remain two of its most profitable businesses. The town today is doing well for itself and will continue to flourish, despite the still-frigid winters. (Cohen, Cohen et al. 2003)

After dawdling over coffee, 10:30 finally arrived, and we met Andy at the beginning of the Trail.

"You ready, big guy?" I flashed him a grin.

"As ready as I'll ever be. Did you bring duct tape?"

"First thing I packed. You read the sign yet?"

A kiosk nearby announced the 'Western Terminus.' In many of the larger towns along the Trail were kiosks, some so new it appeared they were completed within minutes of our arrival, which provided condensed versions of the information on our maps. Although we learned little from them ourselves, we found them to be a great way to reach out to the local public, and to visitors passing through, and we often encountered others reading and discussing them.

We did our last minute organization, leaving some extra food with Elizabeth who we would see again in a week. She lives outside of Plattsburgh, New York, which the NFCT travels through so she had offered us a place to stay when we got there (not that I would have given her much choice). Then we loaded the boat with everything, and stood looking at it affectionately for half a beat.

"Alright Andy, you set? Are we ready? Now is as good a time as any."

Andy shook his head, "I can't believe we are actually starting. We've been talking about this for so long. And now it's here. Let's go! I want to paddle!"

The requisite pictures, hugs, and final kisses finally took place and then we were off! The first stroke felt like a dream. I reached far in front of me and dug in, ripping the surface with my paddle. The canoe shot ahead, gliding smoothly across the lake. Andy in front of me was pulling strongly as well and we swerved back and forth slightly before getting our rhythm.

"On the road again…Just can't wait to be on the road again," I sang and Andy hummed along for a bit before joining in. We both were ecstatic and filled with joy to finally be on our way.

The early morning mist had already burned off, and we quickly paddled around the bend, showing off for the ladies we were leaving behind, before slowing to a more manageable pace for the remainder of the day. We planned to travel only partway through the Fulton Chain of Lakes, a system of lakes connected by dams northeast of Old Forge. It was a gorgeous day, and we made great time, passing loons, families of ducklings, and several deer, one of whom was eating grass while standing on a private dock in front of a summer cottage. The owners were not around, and the deer seemed to be content. He certainly ignored us.

We stopped for lunch at a public beach, and Andy decided to swim out to a buoy perhaps 200 yards out. He did so, only to find when he tried to tread water next to the buoy that he was in waist deep water. He looked a little foolish, and I had a good laugh at his expense from shore.

Right next to the beach writer and paddler George Washington Sears camped, though it must have been a little wilder when he paddled by in 1883. Going by the pen name "Nessmuk", he paddled 266 miles from Booneville (near Old Forge) to Paul Smith's College and back, chronicling his adventures in the magazine *Forest and Stream*. We would trace part of his journey for our first several days of paddling. Many years later in 1990 Christine Jerome stopped on this very beach while retracing his paddle, chronicling her trip in <u>An Adirondack Passage</u>.(Jerome 1994) I will leave Nessmuk's adventures to her able pen, but I enjoyed the thought of us tracing her tracing his journey. These waterways have been traveled by many and will be traveled by many more in future years to come.

Our first portage ran between Fifth and Sixth Lakes. We had little trouble, portaging the .4 miles in perhaps half an hour, taking two trips to transport our boat and gear. We used wannigans to store our food and common gear, and thick, rubber dry-bags for our personal gear. Wannigans have a long and distinguished history. Simply wooden boxes constructed of pine boards, they have been used in Canada and northern New England for hundreds of years.(Conover 1991) Often regarded today as traditional and outdated, I find them to be a remarkably efficient and effective way to carry gear on a canoe trip. They have an amazing array of uses from storage to camp table to seat to stepping stool. Extremely durable, they are able to survive a long canoe journey in near-pristine shape. While not waterproof, this is easily compensated for with the advent of Ziploc bags. Finally, they are extremely efficient on the portage trail for carrying heavy loads of a large size. To do this, we used tumplines.

Tumplines are perhaps the single most important piece of equipment carried on a canoe journey involving portages besides the canoe and paddles themselves. Used by nearly all native cultures that carried loads over distances, they allow one to carry phenomenal loads with ease (the record being a figure north of 1,200 pounds – though it is doubtful that *that* load was done with ease). Given their importance, it is surprising that they are little more than a long leather strap. Using simple knots they are tied around a wannigan, leaving a three foot loop with headpiece hanging loose. This is then placed over the top of the head, near the hairline. By leaning slightly forward when walking, all the weight within the wannigan is transported through the neck into the back. The wannigan's flat lid allows the portager to load additional bags and gear on top. The spine is naturally aligned to avoid injury, and great weights feel insignificant. It is the most efficient way, by far, of carrying heavy loads over long distances along canoe carries, yet the technique has fallen into disuse.(Conover 1991) Only a few old-timers still employ the method, and only the oldest canoe camps still teach it (including the one at which I learned to canoe). I also used a tumpline on the canoe which, tied together with two paddles, takes much of the weight off the shoulders and instead also directs it into the neck and back, making it easier to portage long distances. The longest portage of the Northern Forest Canoe Trail, slightly under 6 miles, felt like a breeze when I employed a tumpline, and this first one into Sixth Lake was straightforward as well.

I don't mind portaging, and in fact enjoy walking with a canoe over my head. It is a nice change from paddling, and serves to break up the day. There is something meditative about carrying a canoe. It creates a sort of cone of silence over you, and I just let my mind wander as I walk along. Even mosquitos seem to avoid canoe portagers – perhaps their tribute to the traditional method of portaging. It can be very peaceful, and with a well-tied tumpline, I only need to shift the boat once in a while to change where the pressure is on my head and shoulders.

By taking one load of gear across the portage, walking back empty-handed, and then taking a second load across, we walked three times the distance of the actual portage, but that can not be helped on a canoe trip. If you aren't using wheels to portage (we most emphatically were *not*), then you have no choice but to take two loads. We consciously chose to go wheel-less, just like we consciously chose to use old-fashioned wannigans and travel by canoe. We were traveling through history - becoming part of history ourselves, if only on a small scale - and to our way of thinking that meant doing it the old way. We could better understand past travels by imitating their methods. Besides, we ourselves knew no other way, and we certainly were not in a rush to get anywhere anyways.

We paddled across Sixth and Seventh Lakes, passing a group of men and women in dive gear (removing invasive species from the lake bed) to arrive at our campsite on an island at the end of Seventh Lake around four o'clock. We relaxed for a bit before collecting wood and cooking dinner. Since it was our first day out of town, we ate fresh steak. Andy soon proved to be a wizard with campfire cooking, and he could cook steak, hamburgers, hot dogs, whatever to perfection. Thank God, because my typical fare involves more black than red when it comes to fresh meat.

We were camped on the east side of the island, so we bushwhacked to the west side to watch the sunset. Our first night of the trip, and we were both feeling strong after a good day.

"Thanks for coming Andy. It's good to have you around. That steak wasn't too bad, eh?"

"No kidding. You suppose every night will be like this?"

"Well…we might have rain *occasionally*. But I figure the weather gods will be friendly to us."

"Hell of a sunset. Hell of a way to end the first day. It doesn't get much better than this."

I just shook my head. No response was needed. The sunset spoke for itself.

The mural of reds, oranges, yellows, and purples that filled the sky in front of us only served to heighten the sense that the coming trip was going to be a good one. The doubts that had filled my mind only that morning had disappeared with the first paddle strokes of the day, and only serenity filled me now. The sunset seemed to embody a good omen for the trip to come and we went to bed with our thoughts on the journey to come in the following days and weeks.

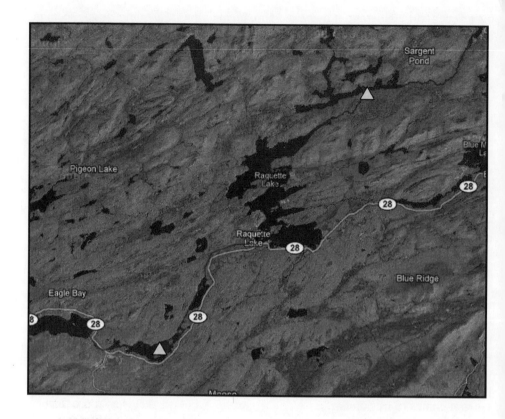

June 6th, Day 2 – Seventh Lake to Forked Lake: I awoke the next morning only to find that I had packed whole beans instead of ground coffee. As any coffee drinker knows, a morning without coffee is terrible. Needless to say, I was nigh on furious with myself, but managed to make do with only oatmeal.

We packed up and paddled for perhaps five minutes before coming to our first portage of the day. We carried through a campground for one mile with little trouble, and then after crossing Eighth Lake, carried another 1.3 miles. We caught up to four men who were doing the same portages we were, out for a couple days journey. They were wheeling their canoes however, and we enjoyed a little friendly ribbing from them about our mode of portaging.

"You know it's a lot easier if you don't carry the damn thing."

"Psshaw. You fellas are moving pretty slow. Why don't you take a break and I'll come back and carry your canoes for you," I retorted

They snorted. "Deal. We'll even toss in a couple of beers for you as well."

Just then one of the wheels got caught on a root and I left them behind me, cursing at all trees in general. Wheeling a canoe is all fine and good on a clear, open trail, but when it comes to thin, meandering trails over rocks and logs or bushwhack portages, wheels just don't cut it. You need to *carry* the canoe. That is why a 'portage' is also called a 'carry'. And while most (but not all) of the carries on this trip were wheel-able, we had specifically agreed pre-trip to do it the old way. We *wanted* to carry the canoe, to use wannigans, and to eschew wheels. This was a historic route, and we wanted to embody that history as we traveled.

I motored along on this portage as well. The trail was fine, weaving in and out of trees and well managed. Others argue that carrying the canoe is tough but it's really just putting one foot in front of the other – just like walking except with a canoe on your head. To me, that's a lot easier than getting hung up on every root that crosses your path. The nice weather had continued and red-winged blackbirds chirped in the swamp, showing their red banners occasionally as we walked past. What a day for a paddle and portage!

This second portage ended with a brand-new boardwalk through a swamp out into a small stream, Brown's Tract Inlet (named for the original owner of much of this area and the founder of what is now Old Forge).(Donaldson 2001) We paddled downstream several miles through twisting swamplands before arriving in beautiful Raquette Lake, though not without crossing several beaver dams. Beaver dams, as long as they are low, are a source of great entertainment if you are using a sturdy ABS (a plastic composite) boat (which we were). Starting fifty feet away, we would yell, "Ramming speed!" paddle our hardest, and cruise over the top of the dam, splashing down on the other side. This works fine as long as the change in water level is no more than several feet. A larger drop, however, results in the boat tipping sideways and occupants and gear spilling out - entertaining in its own right, but usually not an end goal.

I had built the wannigans at home before starting, but apparently the nails I had used in the bottom were not long enough, because the bottoms began to separate from the sides with the weight of all the food we had. We decided a quick stop in the hamlet of Raquette Lake was in order, so we pulled up. It indeed was a hamlet, with general store, library, post office, bar, and not much else. It was also quite empty.

The town (originally on the other side of the lake) was founded by W.W. Durant, a name that one cannot help but run across throughout the Adirondacks. His father created a railroad empire which Durant inherited. The family businesses also included several steamships, many of the "Great Camps" or hotels of the Adirondacks, and vast land-holdings. Unfortunately for Durant, the end of the Gilded Age was not kind to him and his fortune gradually slipped away at the turn of the century, due in part to a lawsuit brought by his sister and the death of a large and benevolent creditor. He turned to managing the Great Camps he had once owned, sometimes employed by his own former employees. Some of his buildings and camps still stand. Raquette Lake, however, seems to have fallen on hard times as well, though we were assured that hordes of tourists passed through in the summer months.(Kaiser 1986)

We stopped in the general store first, buying coffee (thank God), cokes, chips, and receiving a dozen nails *gratis*. Then we found a spot of grass and enjoyed lunch in the shade while watching motorcycles cruise through town. This proved to be a pattern – motorcycles were pretty much everywhere and there were always groups cruising through the small towns we stopped in. Probably the main patronage of this general store, and the reason it is still around, since there appeared to be little else nearby. Certainly they were what kept the bar up and running, since we doubted that canoeists were the big drinkers.

We stopped in at the little local library before leaving town, and met the librarian who was very friendly in a distant way. I asked her about the town's history. She replied with "Oh, there is a ton of history around here." I waited for her to elaborate, but she was clearly done, so we left with no more information than that. I was forced to look it up myself later

Perhaps the most interesting character of this area was Alvah Dunning, a well-known hermit-guide, who haunted this neighborhood including Eighth Lake, Brown's Tract Inlet, and Raquette Lake. He hunted and trapped on these waters throughout much of the nineteenth century, alternately impressing and infuriating visitors. Known for his stubbornness and eccentricity, he refused to abide by many of the laws and hunted, fished, and camped where he pleased. When told that the world was a sphere and that it rotated on an axis, he would hold up a cup of water, turn it over, and say, "Ain't that what wud happen to yer lakes and rivers if yer turned 'em upside down? I ain't believin' no such tommyrot as that!"(Donaldson 2002) As increasing numbers of tourists visited the area, he moved around in search of solitude, though it rarely stayed with him for long. He died in 1902 from asphyxiation when the hotel he was staying in (one of the few times he slept indoors in his entire life) had a gas leak.(Donaldson 2002)

A short portage brought us into Forked Lake. We planned to stay at a lean-to on Forked Lake, but after paddling past where it was shown to be on the map, we saw no sign of it, so we stayed at a clearing which held an outhouse, fire pit, and collapsed shed. It was unmarked on our maps but it served our purposes admirably. Perhaps it was an old hunting camp. It was clearly unused though, with no recent fires and branches littering the area. Collecting firewood was a simple task this evening.

I used a wannigan lid and drew a checkerboard on it, then took a stick and cut slices off it, like a stick of pepperoni, for checkers. I stained half of them with ash from the fire, and voila! A checkerboard set. It provided great entertainment most nights as we digested our meal over the embers of the cooking fire. The opening night saw me take the prize, two games to Andy's one.

The first of many repairs also came this night. I flipped the wannigans over and drove the new, longer nails into the bottom, securing it. The wannigan bottoms never again gave us trouble, but other repairs and adjustments were needed on many evenings. Even if I was only adjusting my tumpline because it had loosened from use, it seemed as though the repairs were un-ending. It kept us busy, but I think that repairs are peculiar only to canoe trips. None of my previous hiking trips have engendered a fraction of the repairs required on this trip. Perhaps the homemade wannigans were the cause, or the beating we would give our canoe in the future, but repairs seemed to plague us. We didn't let it bother us. There are more important things to lose sleep over than repairs.

We quickly fell into an evening routine. Upon arriving at camp we would each set up our tents and then put the tarp up together. We would change into dry clothes (as long as it wasn't still raining) and then collect firewood, putting it under the tarp along with the wannigans. Most days, we went right into cooking dinner, but sometimes we would have time in between to read, nap, or simply rest. After having been in the boat all day together, whatever it was, it was usually solitary since we had had enough of each other during the day. Dinner finished, we would fill the pot, frying pan, and our dishes with water. Letting them sit to clean themselves a bit (what I call the 'soap cycle' at home), we would play checkers before digging a cat-hole and cleaning them. Then a small dessert (usually a couple Hershey's kisses or a candy bar) and journal writing and reading in front of the fire. While perhaps not the most electrifying of evenings, it worked well for both of us, and I never felt bored or let down. We were usually too tired for more strenuous activity anyways after a full day of paddling, and it was rare for us to stay up past sunset.

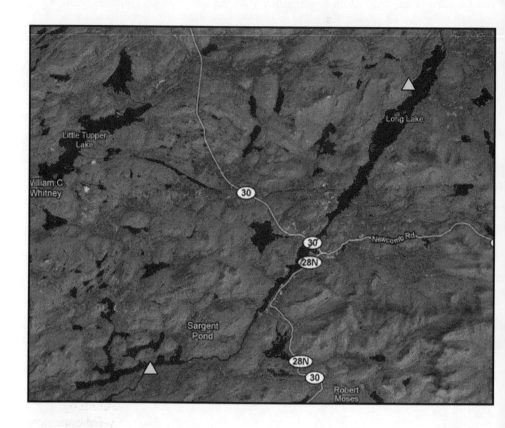

June 7th, Day 3 – Forked Lake to Long Lake: The coffee this morning was almost unbearably delicious. My first coffee in two whole days! O thank God for those luscious, tasty beans. I spent the morning singing an ode to coffee while paddling, Andy shaking his head in disgust.

> O coffee, brown and bitter,
> You wake me up nice and quick,
> Ready for a brand new day,
> It's better than being beaten with a stick.

Pure poetry. Andy wasn't a caffeine addict like me, so he didn't understand. He also didn't seem to have an appreciation for good poetry. Poor un-caffeinated, un-cultured guy!

The morning routine also materialized quickly. I am an early riser, and was often up by five or five-thirty, puttering around camp, building a fire and making breakfast. I enjoyed sitting and slowly sipping my coffee, while looking out over the river, lake, stream, whatever we happened to be camped on, and watching the world wake up with me. My favorite mornings were the ones where, when I awoke, the whole earth appeared to be covered in a dense fog. I would make breakfast amid the heavy dew of morning, and then watch as the rising sun slowly burned off all the mist, and a bright, beautiful, cheery day dawned. I could feel the newness of the day, and all the adventure that could come with it, stealing over me as I sat and watched that yellow orb rise steadily and majestically above me. The crispness of the air, and the bite of the cold, still lingering from the night before, instilled a strong sense of freshness in me, a sense of wonder at the day to come and all that it might hold. Morning is by far my favorite time of day.

Andy on the other hand, hated waking up. He would have slept the day away if I had let him. I would wake him up when I was finished enjoying my morning, usually around seven or seven-thirty. He took very little time and after stuffing a couple of Pop-Tarts into his mouth and taking down his tent he would be ready to go, though he might not be fully awake yet.

We got on the Raquette River today, portaging a short distance around the dam at the head, then paddling several miles down some very bumpy Class II rapids. Several stories are posited for Raquette River's namesake, from the pile of abandoned snowshoes (*raquettes* in French) found on its bank, to the snowshoe shape of a meadow near its mouth, to the hunting for moose done on snowshoes along its banks. It could perhaps even be a corruption of the word "racket" or noise, which the river's rapids certainly made a lot of.(Donaldson 2001)

It was very nice to be moving downstream for much of the morning though. Gravity is a beautiful thing. There were perhaps a dozen fly-fishermen on the river, and they all paused and waved as we went by. They seemed to be looking expectantly at us, as if waiting for us to spill, but we navigated the rapids successfully, if not without a scratch or two. Sorry to disappoint them, but then again, not terribly so.

Another short portage around Buttermilk Falls: a rather large falls for this smaller stretch of river. We took pictures in front, posing on a rather slippery rock at its base. Andy almost fell in, but managed to catch himself.

I mock-scolded him, "You big idiot! Don't die! We've barely started, and already you're going to split your head open."

Andy did a little jig as a retort and nearly fell again before getting down sheepishly. I could only shake my head and mutter, "Dear God."

"Adirondack" Murray, an eccentric minister and writer of the late nineteenth century, told a famous story about "Phantom Falls", often thought to be Buttermilk Falls, in which he and his guide chased a phantom Indian woman over them, only to lose her when their boat flipped. According to the story, however, they made it over the falls unharmed, if soaking wet. If indeed "Phantom Falls" is Buttermilk Falls then they must indeed have had otherworldly help in surviving without a scratch, but perhaps the phantom Indian woman took pity on them and aided their descent. I can only say that we saw no sign of her.(Murray 1970)

Just past Buttermilk Falls was an even bumpier set of rapids. The map recommended portaging during low waters, but we of course ignored that recommendation. The results were not terrible. While not the prettiest run I've ever had, we did make it down. However, a rock jumped right in front of the boat at one point, and we T-boned it at speed (hit it squarely, head-on). Our poor boat now had a dented bow.

But we made it down to Long Lake. We paddled several miles before stopping in the Village of Long Lake. It was Sunday and much of the town, including the general store, was closed. Fortunately, we weren't trying to buy supplies. As we ate lunch, we watched the local float plane service take a duo up for a tour-by-sky of the region. Even though the day was overcast, we agreed that that would be an enjoyable way to spend the afternoon. A quick check on the price proved that it was beyond our budget, however, so we paddled on.

The clouds thickened as we continued down the lake, and spurts of rain began to fall. Mist rolled in as we paddled harder, hoping to reach the end of the lake before it really set in. I resisted donning my rain jacket for as long as possible, but finally had to give in.

"Those damned rain gods. I thought they were going to take a break for the next month!"

"I hope it doesn't rain too hard. Starting a fire could be tough if it starts to pour."

"Ehh, we'll be alright. With my unbelievable skills at building a teepee and you're fire-breathing power we should be able to do it."

Andy laughed, "O ya, I forgot about that power. I knew there was a reason you wanted me on this trip. And I thought it was my sparkling personality."

"Little did you know."

We made it to 'Camp Riverdale', the lean-to we planned on spending the night at. Camp Riverdale was a summer camp that closed in 1964. The state acquired the lands in 1979 and in accordance with the New York "Forever Wild" clause of the state constitution the buildings were demolished (New York State Archives 2010). After setting up camp, we explored the area to see if we could find any remnants of the camp. I discovered a stone wall built into the bank of the lake, built to hold it up and slow erosion. There were also the remains of an old dock, and Andy found a pit where an outhouse had once stood, but we failed to discover any more about Camp Riverdale.

Across the lake from us, however, was a lean-to called Plumley's Landing, which is located on the site of the home of Mitchell Sabattis, an extremely well-known Abenaki Adirondack guide. The Plumleys (John Plumley was "Adirondack" Murray's guide when they paddled over "Phantom Falls") stayed with him when they first came to the area (Donaldson 2001). They went on to found the town of Long Lake with 8 other families, and it became a hub of the growing timber industry. Logs were floated down to mills both to the north in the St. Lawrence Valley and the east in the Champlain valley where they used for lumber, paper, and other timber needs.

We ate macaroni and cheese topped with corned beef hash. An odd combination, one might think, but we found it to be delicious and it became a staple of the dinner menu for the trip.

We pitched our tents inside the lean-to to keep them dry, taking over the whole lean-to in the process. This perhaps exemplifies one of the big differences between canoeing and hiking in America's parks. When hiking, if you choose to stay at a lean-to, they are regarded as public places, and you should expect several other strangers to join you for the night, setting their sleeping bags up next to yours, and sharing the dryness of the lean-to. If in a popular spot, you should expect the lean-to to be filled, or even over-filled (especially on a rainy night). By the end of the night, these hikers who you have never met before will have become, if not friends, at least known to you. Conversation will abound, and you will find out the life history of your bunk mates, perhaps more than you want to know. Hiking is very much a group activity, and unless you pitch your tent off in the bushes away from everything, you can expect little privacy.

Canoeing, on the other hand, is very much a solo activity. If you stop at a marked campsite on the side of the lake, that campsite is now yours. Even if there are only two of you, like we were doing, once you have stopped at that campsite, the whole lean-to is yours, and only very rarely will someone join you. Much more frequently they will see your boat pulled up on the side, and move on, looking for an unoccupied spot. Rarely do two unknown groups spend the night together, and even out on the open water, conversation appears to be frowned upon. Beyond the passing 'hello,' and perhaps a 'where are you heading?' little is said. Hikers will stop and chat, spending five, ten fifteen minutes or more, talking, perhaps eating a snack together. Canoeists move on, looking for more solitary spots. I do not elevate one system over another, but I have found it a stark contrast and almost universally consistent on my trips, both canoeing and hiking. The one time I shared a lean-to site with another party on a canoe trip, I got some odd looks from the original habitants. They were less than interested in sharing their space and so I pitched my tent away from theirs. We did not interact that evening and I left early the next morning. That interaction would never have occurred in a lean-to along a hiking trail.

The night turned cold and we went to sleep bundled in our clothes, lulled by the soft pitter patter of rain on the roof of the lean-to.

Andy offered, "If only we had a woman to snuggle up to and keep us warm on nights like these, perhaps even give us a massage."

"If only…" I responded, and that night I dreamt of warm women.

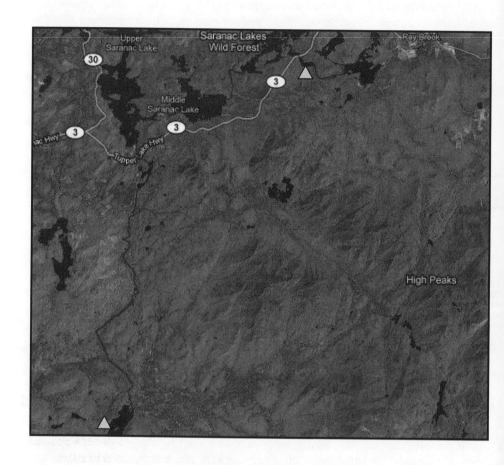

June 8th, Day 4 – Long Lake to Second Pond: We awoke to a cold, thick mist covering the lake. However, as it often does, the sun cleared it out by early morning, and a beautiful, sunny day dawned with blue skies and warmth. We joined the Raquette River again where it left Long Lake and paddled gently downstream with the current.

We passed Cold River, up which another hermit, Noah Rondeau, lived. He would perhaps have been relegated to obscurity like so many other hermits (doubtlessly how many of them would want it) but for an invitation he accepted in 1947. The New York Conservation Department air-dropped an invitation to Rondeau, asking him to speak at the Sportsmen's Show in New York City. He replied in the affirmative and went on to tour sportsmen's shows for four whirlwind years, speaking in favor of wilderness conservation. A monument still supposedly stands on the site of his original hut, though we did not venture up to see it (De Sormo 1975).

Hermits and the Adirondacks seem to have an affinity for each other, and we found more in residence here than anywhere else on the Trail (two others once lived in close proximity to each other on Long Lake). Why the Adirondacks, I'm not sure, but they certainly picked a beautiful spot to spend their days in solitude. As a wilderness lover myself, I can certainly sympathize with their pleasure in natural beauty, if not their self-enforced exile from society. Humans are social creatures, I will be the first to admit, and without other humans to interact with humans, like bread, become stale. I also believe that, like many things, contrast is what creates true enjoyment. There can be no joy without despair, no happiness without the sad, and no appreciation for nature's splendor if you aren't also aware of the noise, hubbub, and pollution of cities.

I do, however, happen to have a hermit in my family tree. John Turner Brakeley, my first cousin four times removed, was born in 1847 in New Jersey. He graduated from Princeton in 1869, enrolled in law school the next year, and seemed to be headed towards a career in law and marriage to a beautiful girl (history has lost her name). However, one fateful evening he saw his fiancé in the arms of another man. She re-avowed her love for John Turner Brakeley but he, not believing her, turned to solitude. He became a hermit in 1873. He established himself at Layaway Plantation, a nearby, deserted village in the pine barrens of New Jersey, and remained there for the rest of his life. His father owned the building and surrounding land and, although surprised, permitted his son to do as he chose. Visitors were permitted as long as they did not gawk, but sooner or later (often sooner) it would be hinted that they had worn out their welcome and should move on. He preferred the solitude (Beck 1961).

He did not remain idle, nor, like many of his wilder counterparts, fill his time with hunting, trapping, or guiding. He instead devoted himself to science. In one room he set up five desks in a circle, each desk filled with his paperwork and research. The weather, wind, stars, insects, birds, flowers, and much of nature became his subjects. Nearby cranberry bogs fascinated him. Wasps in particular seemed to hold his fancy and he invented the technique of pouring Plaster of Paris into their burrows to map their subterranean homes. He cultivated many species of flowers in surrounding gardens, and water lilies in a nearby pond. He may even have imported the first carp to the state from Germany (Beck 1961).

All this solitude, however, did not detract from his sense of humor. When asked about his matrimonial prospects he described them as, "below par but with an upward tendency," although whom he thought he was going to marry at this point in his life I'm not sure (Brakeley 2010).

His research efforts were largely destroyed when he died around 1912. His remaining family, perhaps embarrassed by their kinship with a hermit, destroyed much of his notes and research upon his passing. He lives on, however, in a short chapter in the book, Forgotten Towns of Southern New Jersey by Henry Charlton Beck, in much of my grandmother's research and notes, and in the names of several species. A mosquito he discovered is named for him, the

Corethrella brakeleyi, and a fern as well. Little remains of Layaway (Beck 1961). So perhaps there may be a little hermit in me after all.

We portaged around Raquette Falls, using our return trip for the second load to avoid the portage trail and instead rock-hop up the river to look at the falls. We found an old cable still with one end embedded in rock which may have been part of the old dam once here. Adirondack guides blew the dam up, as well as the newest steamboat owned by W. W. Durant, the *Buttercup*, in protest of the business the new technology was stealing from them. They, like the Luddites and all others who have tried to halt the unstoppable train called 'progress', failed in the long run. Travel and business would, of course, modernize the area. The dam, however, was never rebuilt, and for that I thank those guides. They were never caught (Hochschild 1962).

Directly below Raquette Falls was the site of Mother Johnson's house. Lucy Johnson and her husband Philander were the first residents in this area and ran a simple inn/hostel for travelers. Known for their heartiness and kindness, they were immortalized by "Adirondack" Murray when he passed through and told his readers to "never go by Mother Johnson's without tasting her pancakes, and, when you leave, leave with her an extra dollar"(Murray 1970). They, like many of the first residents including Alvah Dunning and Noah Rondeau, followed their stomachs instead of the game laws, as the following interchange between Mother Johnson and 1874 visitor Seneca Ray Stoddard demonstrates.

"'What kind of fish is that, Mrs. Johnson?' I inquired

'Well,' said she, 'they don't have no name after the 15th of September. They are a good deal like trout, but it's against the law to catch trout after the fifteenth, you know.'"(Stoddard 1983)

We looked, but could find no sign of their log cabin. Time and weather have no doubt reduced it to dust.

The Raquette River was a beautiful river. It was undeveloped, and much of its banks were protected lands. Trees lined the water, leaning over and shading much of our paddle. Grasses swayed gently in the breeze as birds flitted in and out of the underbrush. Families of ducks, the young small and innocent, splashed and fled before us. As our trip continued and summer began, we were able to watch the ducklings grow and develop, until by the end they were nearly as large as their parents and beginning to grow in their adult feathers. A blue heron led us downstream, always keeping 100 yards in front of the canoe. Fish swam lazily beneath our paddles, safe in the knowledge that we could do little without fishing tackle. We watched a bald eagle land on a tree almost directly above, and took several good photographs of him watching us. He didn't seem to mind our presence either and rested awhile before taking off. It was a disappointment to have to leave this river.

We paddled up the short and windy Stony Creek, getting sidetracked once but soon managing to find Stony Creek Pond. Portaging across Indian Carry (known as the 'Times Square' of the woods for its long use and popularity

(Jamieson 1981)) into Upper Saranac Lake, we faced an abrupt change. Where the Raquette had had no development and Stony Creek Pond only a few houses, Upper Saranac Lake was clearly a vacation destination. Modern mansions lined much of the shore, and motorboats plied the waters. A big difference and certainly not one for the better.

We did, however, run into Walter, Trail Director of the Northern Forest Canoe Trail and Nick, who was helping him out. They were working with a New York Department of Conservation employee, Steve, to scout out the site of a future campsite, and discuss destroying some buildings on a recently acquired piece of property. After handshakes were shared around, discussion moved to this year's thru-paddlers.

"Well we're just happy to meet some thru-paddlers out on the trail. It's great to know that we are doing all this work for a purpose, and that people are using the Trail!" Walter was thrilled we were out paddling.

"Do you know of anyone else thru-paddling this year?" Andy asked.

"Why yes. There are two thru-kayakers out in front of you, perhaps a week and two weeks ahead. And I heard about some guy who was stand-up paddling."

"Was his name Shaggy?" There had been some entries in a couple of log books placed on portages by a paddler named Shaggy who seemed to be attempting a thru-paddle, and I thought it might be him.

"I believe so."

"And you said he is stand-up paddling? Why would he do that? What is the purpose of paddling while standing up? Isn't that a pain in the butt?" Andy asked

Walter laughed, "You know, I'm not sure. I haven't actually seen him, I just heard about it. You'd think he'd have a tough time with whitewater and heavy winds and such, so maybe he only does it sometimes. I don't know."

"Anything we should know about the trail ahead?"

"Nope. It's pretty well marked. Just make sure you go through the locks – they are pretty neat."

"Thanks Walter and Nick! Keep up the good work, and thanks for the news!"

Still dubious over Shaggy's method of paddling, we vowed to keep an eye out for him. We never did see him. To each his own, however, and if that's the way he enjoyed paddling, then it was all right with us.

Fortunately we were only on the over-developed Upper Saranac for a short time before we portaged across Bartlett's Carry (named for a nearby hotel built in 1854 (Donaldson 2001)) into Middle Saranac. No houses were here, and we wound our way between islands before entering the Saranac River. We went through the Upper Locks which dropped us down perhaps five feet to the level of Lower Saranac Lake. Sitting in the canoe, holding onto the slimy ropes on the side of the lock as the water level visibly fell around us made me feel rather small. But the ranger didn't seem to mind that she had to operate the lock for only a canoe, and we paddled onwards. We arrived at our campsite just past six o'clock, having put in a full ten hours on the water and covering 27 miles including 2.5 miles of carries. We had covered a lot of mileage which felt really good (although my shoulders didn't really think so).

While the day had begun with gorgeous weather, by the time we camped it had clouded over and rain was threatening. We made dinner of rice and beans while the wind blew harder, feeling and tasting of rain to come. We managed to settle in for the night, however, before it started, and remained snug all night long while the rain pounded down on our tents and tarp.

It was times like these that I really got to thinking about just what life might have in store for me. As I laid there in the tent with the pitter-patter of rain dripping, I couldn't help but wonder just how many more nights I was going to get to spend in the wilderness. Am I going to be forced to steal a weekend here, a night there, treasuring my few vacation days, or will I continue to be able to take long trips like this one? I drifted off to sleep, wondering. In the end, it would be up to me, but life is a long road, and who knows what barriers might jump in my way.

Chapter 2: The Saranac River

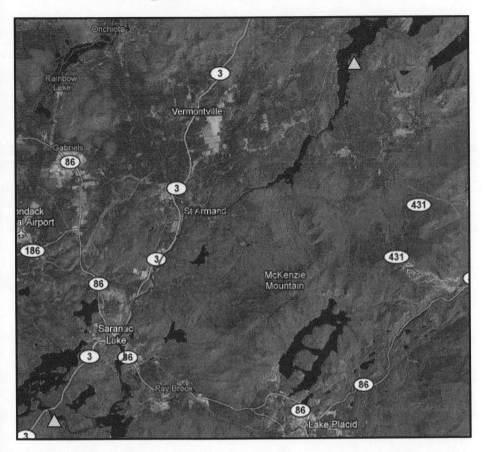

June 9th, Day 5 – Second Pond to Union Falls Pond: We awoke to a light rain. The Town of Saranac Lake was only a few miles away, so we had decided to skip breakfast in favor of a real one in town. I built a fire anyways and brewed some coffee. Rain schmain. I needed my coffee.

The rain slowed as we paddled out and stopped soon after. Another beautiful day in New York. We paddled through the Lower Locks, briefly chatting with the ranger running them.

"Where'd you guys stay last night?"

Andy answered, "On the point back there."

"The one right across from the ranger station?"

"Yup."

"Just past the bridge, right? You had a blue tarp up, right?"

Slightly puzzled now as to why he was so curious, I agreed in the affirmative again.

"Oh okay. Have a good day." He gave a little smile as we paddled on. I didn't realize why until we were through the locks.

When I use the outhouse, I prefer to keep the door open, as long as it is not directly facing the campsite. It gives me a breeze, some light, and makes the whole experience that much more pleasant. This particular morning, it happened to have a clear view of the pond, which I was enjoying immensely when a motorboat cruised by, driven by a lone man (the ranger, I now realized). He and I looked at each other for the two seconds it took for him to pass, staring but doing little else. I, being rarely embarrassed, thought little of it until I pondered his questioning, and realized he was the man in the motorboat, on his way to work at the lock. He seemed to get a kick out of realizing it was me with my pants around my ankles on the john.

We crossed Oseetah Lake, named for a local Saranac legend. Oseetah was a beautiful bird who a young warrior, Blazing Sun, was in love with. Blazing Sun, however, was engaged to the chief's daughter, so Oseetah fled to avoid the scandal. Blazing Sun discovered her, and tried to convince her to fly away with him. Oseetah instead hurled herself from a cliff to preserve both their honor. However, water lilies bloomed where she landed, the first ever seen, and it was clear to all the Saranac Indians that Oseetah had returned to this life as a water lily, with a flower of white, symbolizing her purity, and yellow, symbolizing her great love (Northern Forest Canoe Trail 2005).

The Town of Saranac Lake has several public docks, where we tied our boat and strolled into town. It is a pleasant village, clearly geared towards tourists, and has a bustling main street that was already busy with people despite the early hour and slight drizzle. It was certainly a far cry from a "miserable hamlet" as it was described by one resident in 1877 (Donaldson 2001). We bought a newspaper to see what news we had been missing (nothing) and ate a massive breakfast at the local café. Pancakes, French Toast, eggs, home fries, sausage, and bacon all disappeared and we had to remain sitting for another fifteen minutes after the stuffing before we could budge. A local woman stopped by, hearing our conversation about the Trail, and congratulated us on getting this far. It was always great to know that people are aware of the Trail, since we thought it was relatively unknown. We found throughout its length that a fair number of locals knew of it, and some had even helped to build its portage trails.

It took us a bit to find the grocery store, but we finally did, where we resupplied. On our way back to the boat, we passed a medical center with a plaque out front as a tribute to Dr. Edward Livingston Trudeau, and his son and grandson. Dr. Trudeau had established a tuberculosis research center here when he found his own TB improving with the clean mountain air. Thousands were treated at the sanatorium including the famous author, Robert Louis Stevenson, of Treasure Island fame (Donaldson 2001).

The Saranac River below town twisted and wound its way through marshy swampland. It, like the Raquette River, was one of the many rivers used to float timber down to construction-happy cities. How the massive logs managed to make it down the sluggish and twisty rivers without getting hung up repeatedly remains a mystery to me, but make it down they did, and often enough to make several men quite rich.

The majority of lumbermen, however, were the lumberjacks, drovers, edgers and other woodsmen who cut, de-limbed, and floated the logs downriver to the mill. They lived tough lives working long hours in the woods with little pay. Today their job has often been romanticized but in reality it was exhausting, dangerous work, and a vast array of injuries has been widely-documented. Trees seemed to have a habit of dropping branches onto the unwary, logs would suddenly come lose from a log jam and crush the drivers, or a tired logger would forget the cigarette in his mouth and burn down the bunkhouse. One incident that immediately gained renown was the case of George Lanz in 1906. A thirteen-foot piece of spruce was ejected from a saw and pierced him clean through his body sideways, pinning one of his arms to his side and exiting partway out his back. His fellow crewmembers cut off the protruding parts, brought him to the doctor, and before he knew it he was back on the job. Many, however, were not as lucky as he (Welsh 1995).

Hundreds of birds sang and chirped around us, and we identified the red-winged blackbird, a vireo, robins, and many others. We also saw great blue heron, a muskrat, and several families of ducks. The mother ducks had several ways of trying to protect themselves and their offspring. Sometimes they simply herded their brood out of our path, hiding in among the branches on the far bank. Sometimes they all dove underwater simultaneously, popping back up in a different spot. Some mothers performed the 'wounded duck' facade, flapping their wings uselessly and zigzagging as though confused, until they deemed that we were far enough away from their kids when they would suddenly heel around and flap back to the family. We even saw one duck crouched motionless on the bank within two feet of us as we passed by, trying to blend in with some sparse grass. She stuck out like a sore thumb, but fortunately we weren't in the mood for duck for dinner. What could they have possibly thought we were, anyways? What predator resembles a long, green, slightly beat-up and rather slow-moving canoe? No alligators in the area that I knew of, unless the local zoo recently had a jailbreak. In any case, they remained safe from us.

I had been reading some short stories by Edward Kanze, a local Adirondack naturalist. He describes his house as being on, or nearby, the Saranac River in some of the stories, so we kept an eye out for it, but failed to pick it out from any of the other houses along the bank.

The banks began to get firmer, and the river narrowed as we continued downstream. The marsh grasses were again replaced with hardwoods as the current sped up. We cruised through several smaller Class II rapids, taking on little water, before opening up into Franklin Falls Pond. A short portage around a dam at the end, and we entered Union Falls Pond. The wind had picked up and we battled heavy crosswinds as we paddled to our campsite partway down the Lake.

Our campsite, facing west, received heavy winds all evening, and cooking was difficult since the heat blew nearly sideways. We managed to fry up some burgers along with some freeze-dried corn chowder, however, and settled in for a good meal. As we ate, a rabbit hopped up and gave us the hairy eye-ball for a while, before continuing on with his business. The wind began to die down, however, as we turned in for a good night's rest. The sunset out over the lake was stunning.

June 10ᵗʰ, Day 6 – Union Falls Pond to the Saranac River near Picketts Corners: What a day this one turned out to be. We got back on the river after a short paddle to the end of Union Falls Pond. Early in the day, we passed under five turkey vultures sitting together in a dead tree.

"Looks like they are looking for breakfast."

"They're going to have to wait a long time if they think we're it. I don't plan on dying anytime soon!" Andy *did* look quite healthy just then.

"Good thing, Andy. I don't want to have to paddle this canoe all by myself."

They turned their head slowly in unison as they watched us go by.

"Well, I just hope it isn't some kind of omen."

Several sets of Class IIs got us into the groove to start off, and we conquered those with a bit of dexterity and some good old-fashioned strength. The river grew a little steeper afterwards, however, and the water got a little bigger, becoming Class II+s, long stretches of whitewater with few flat spots to separate the sets. It just kept coming, miles and miles of whitewater. The river was shallow and we were continually scraping bottom with our paddles, struggling to pull enough water to move the boat successfully back and forth across the river to try and stay in the channel and avoid the rocks. Our maps told us that towards mid- to late summer the river becomes too shallow to successfully paddle down it, but it felt like that day was rapidly nearing.

We misread a section, however, and got ourselves into a really rocky section, catching the bow on a boulder and flipping. We managed to drag the boat to shore, with most of the gear still in it, and righted it. Piling back in, we continued on our way.

I will be the first to admit, I get extremely frustrated when I flip in a canoe. As we ate lunch on the side of the river, I was not a happy person. When I'm angry, I don't complain, I don't yell (too much), I simply clam up. Andy tried for pleasant conversation over the food, and I was not having it.

"At least it's warm out. We'll dry quickly."

"Mm."

"And we didn't lose anything. We've got all our food still dry, and our bags are all set and everything."

"Mm."

I was pissed the river had gotten the better of us, and I was not in the mood for chit-chat. Andy generously allowed me to take over stern for the rest of the whitewater (we switched stern and bow daily), since he thought it was he I was mad at. I was just mad in general, at the whole situation. I really don't like to flip.

After lunch we continued on downstream. I as newly elected sternman for the day neglected to read the map as carefully as I should have, and saw only Class IIs further downstream. We continued cruising downstream, again dodging this way and that to avoid rocks and still scraping along the bottom, when we rounded a corner and saw a bit of a drop ahead of us.

Andy called out, 'Heads up! Drop ahead! Let's pull over and scout it.'

I overruled him, shouting, 'The hell with it, we're going!'

'You sure? I think we should check it out...'

'We're hitting it baby, dead center!'

And so we did. It was a Class IV five foot ledge spanning the river. The map had warned us, but we failed to pay attention, and I was feeling particularly gung-ho as newly appointed sternman for the day. With a big 'Yee-Haa!' we went over the edge, submarining immediately. 'Submarining' is when you go over a drop too big for an open boat to handle and, instead of staying above the surface of the water, the bow of the canoe simply goes straight underwater, resulting in immediate submersion beneath the water (much like a submarine will do when diving). We submarined, and found ourselves still in the boat, with water up to our necks, the boat completely submerged. I yelled for Andy to keep steady, that if we could keep balanced then it would be okay. Of course that wasn't true, the boat was pretty much on the bed of the river, and none of the gear or the boat could be seen under the surface of the water. Only our heads, arms and paddles remained above the surface, and I was still paddling like a madman while Andy braced to try to stay balanced. A submerged canoe is extremely unbalanced. Luck was not with us, however, and immediately after the first ledge was a second of another couple feet. Our submerged boat with us in it went over this ledge as well, and we spilled out along with all our gear.

The food wannigan opened up, and all our Ziplocs of food floated off downstream. We again tugged our boat to the side with a little gear still left in it (we had neglected to tie anything down, a mistake we would be doomed to repeat), and righted it, climbing back in. The next mile was an Easter egg hunt for gear and food, us chasing little bags of food back and forth across the river, hitting too many rocks since we were watching for food and gear, and not the river. We found all the gear, and enough food to get us into Plattsburgh, however, and continued on our way, leaving only a little food and my treasured ball cap on the riverbed somewhere. A sacrifice to the river gods.

We had an observer for this second flip as well. A fisherman was standing in his waders, partway out into the stream just below the first ledge. He watched us approach it, argue over scouting it, and then decide to go over. As the bow began to submerge I glanced over and saw him laughing heartily as he watched our futile attempt at running it. We submerged, head and all, and when we popped up, still in the canoe, between the first and second ledges, he was still laughing and cheering us on. When we finally flipped over the second ledge, and I dunked my head again, he was giving us the thumbs-up. That was the last glance I had of him, chuckling and holding out the universal 'Go get 'em, tiger,' as we spilled and spread our gear across the river. We must have been quite a sight as we tried to paddle the submerged canoe. It made his day, I'm sure.

This flip was my fault, so I could only be angry at myself. I had had too good a time going over the ledge, however, and watching that fisherman, so my good spirits returned.

"O man, did you see that?! Yee-Haa! What a way to go baby. That's what I call a flip."

"Did you see the look on that fisherman's face? He loved us!"

Andy, fortunately, had never lost his good humor – in fact I don't think he ever did on the trip – and we reminisced about the ledge for the remainder of the day.

And finally, after miles and miles of tough paddling, the whitewater was pretty much done for the day. We hit two more tough sets of Class III water, with big waves and bigger boulders, but by hugging the shore we got through them. They were short, so even though we took on a fair amount of water, we were able to bail at the end of each.

High Falls Dam creates a 60 foot waterfall which we portaged around towards the end of the day. Below it there is a mile of Class IV and Vs that we also had to portage. It was extremely impressive water, and only experienced kayakers would have been able to run it. We were thankful for the trail around. We also had discovered a number of purple, triangular boxes hanging from trees, all in the vicinity of dams. A little research determined that the boxes have been hung not just near dams but along many of New York's back roads (the only time we were on roads was portaging, and many of our portages were around dams, hence the mistaken association) and are there to help discover if the Emerald Ash Borer beetle has infested the area. The beetle is an invasive species that preys on and kills ash trees, and supposedly they like the color purple. The boxes have also been imbued with the smell of an ash tree in distress (whatever that smells like) to further attract the beetles to it. An interesting way to detect their presence, but whatever works.

We stopped briefly in Redford at a gas station to supplement our meager food supplies. We had had 2-3 days worth of food pre-flip, but now only had enough for dinner and breakfast, so we picked up some crackers for lunch for tomorrow before arriving in Plattsburgh. Just before camping, we passed a sign stating that in its heyday, the Saranac River saw hundreds of thousands of logs each year drifting down to the mills on Lake Champlain. Now it sees 21,000 boats a year (according to the lock ranger we passed the day before). We bush-camped on the side of the river, across from the road and some houses. It was a good spot though, well shielded by some evergreens with good flat spots for tent and plenty of wood for a fire.

I will always prefer bush camping to campsite camping. A bush campsite, while missing a large cleared area for tents and kitchen area and lacking a fire pit and picnic table, feels a lot more like camping. There is none of the trash lying around that often plagues many official campsites, and there is always plenty of wood, since the area has not been picked over. The campsite is also much smaller and the whole set up feels much cozier than an official campsite. And bush camps, by their very definition, exist just about anywhere a tent can fit – there is no need to organize a trip around labeled campsites.

We discussed potential names for our already dented and beaten-up boat over a game of checkers.

"How about Blunt-Nose Betty?"

Andy shook his head, "Too coarse. She is much more delicate than that."

"Flat-Faced Franny?"

"Nope. Sam, you need to be a little gentler than this. Our boat is a beautiful thing, and you can't demean that with a vulgar name. Besides, none of those recognize her strength. Do you see all the battle wounds she has? This little lady has and will put up with a lot of abuse. I was thinking more along the lines of 'The Iron Maiden'."

"Isn't that a little cliché?"

"But it's perfect! She is a beautiful maiden with the strength of iron!"

And so she was dubbed 'The Iron Maiden'

As we lounged after dinner, we suddenly heard voices. We immediately became silent ourselves, and, as we sat perhaps ten feet from the river's edge, five canoes came paddling downstream, passing within thirty feet of us. It was a group of men out practicing for a canoe race, their 'hups' setting a cadence as they switched paddling sides to preserve speed. Our fire was still smoking, and we had tents set up, clothes drying on trees, and a canoe on its side, yet they never saw us. The evergreens hid us well. They returned perhaps an hour later, paddling back upstream through the dusk. It was eerie to think of ourselves in their shoes, and to not realize that someone is watching them from not far away…

June 11th, Day 7 - Saranac River to Plattsburgh: I woke Andy forty-five minutes early this morning to make sure we got to Plattsburgh in time. We paddled a gentle and peaceful six miles before a 1.4 mile portage. It was a nice walk through a residential street before we put in next to a condemned bridge, and paddled literally across the river (about 75 feet) and took out again to portage another .6 miles. It was too bad the bridge wasn't open so we could just portage the whole thing at once. We walked along a massive water pipe, part of the dam outflow, for a while, and wondered at the massive amount of engineering that goes into these structures.

Many of them were built in the early 20th century, between 1905 and 1930, though the Kent Falls Dam around which this portage goes was built in 1991. They were predominantly built for hydropower purposes, unlike some of the earlier dams which were built to facilitate logging interests. They seem to all have different shapes and structures, leading us to question why there isn't one universal form. But I suppose that as technologies change and improve over the years, the structures change. We saw basic concrete dams, dams with what look like flying buttresses, and even a dam that was a massive inflatable tube, which, when inflated held back the water and when deflated allowed the water to pass over it. It looks odd, and we thought it might be inefficient, but it is actually a newer technology, and has proven to be both effective and durable. Unfortunately we did not get to see it in action – it remained inflated the whole time we stood next to it.

Dams are a bittersweet 'green' technology with, to my way of thinking, an emphasis on 'bitter'. While they can produce a sizeable amount of electricity, especially from rivers that have many viable sites, such as the Saranac, and they do reduce fossil fuel use for electricity, they have their own set of environmental demons that come when built. The larger dams hold back millions of gallons of water, flooding river basins and destroying riverside wildlife and ecosystems. Thousands of acres of land can be flooded, and homes and migration routes for animals can be destroyed. Fish can no longer move freely up and down stream, even if fish ladders are installed. They often result in massive silting and erosion problems and chemicals such as mercury can build up in the reservoirs, leading to bio-accumulation of toxics in nearby animals. The threat of failure is ever-present for those living directly downstream of it, and maintenance costs can be high. A small dam powering several business nearby can be an effective way to generate green power, but dams built on a massive scale simply have more cons than pros, and with every dam we portaged around I was reminded of the loss of that section of river. In my humble opinion, it is a rare dam that is a good dam.

However, there was little we could do about them, short of setting a couple charges of dynamite and blowing them sky-high, so we paddled onwards. Six miles of gently Class Is followed the portage, and we flew downstream. Three more dams span the river before Plattsburgh, however, and we were forced to portage them all. Below the final portage the river again steepens, and continuous Class IIs run through the City of Plattsburgh and out into Champlain. The make-up of the riverbed also changed, and huge sheets of rock cross the river, broken up by numerous cracks and ridges lying perpendicular to our course and submerged under only a foot or two of water. Instead of the rocks and boulders that normally make up the bed, we were now faced with these massive rock ridges, something I had never seen before. They made the river extremely difficult to read, and we flitted back and forth across the current trying to avoid the worst of the rocks. We managed the first several miles without difficulty, but fate reared her ugly head, and as we tried to squeeze between two slabs, we clipped one. Andy, off-balance, leaned out over the gunwale of the canoe. But instead of righting himself, or bracing, or just sitting up, as it appeared he could do, he just kept tipping and holding onto the gunwale. I was kneeling in the stern, and kept waiting, and waiting, and waiting for him to get back upright, but he never did, and in slow motion he slowly fell out of the boat, dipping the gunwale and flipping the boat and me with him.

Andy let go of his paddle, and then chased it downstream, leaving me to unload all of the gear (fortunately it stayed in the boat), empty the boat of water, and reload it. I paddled downstream and picked up Andy, only to find him barefoot. He had left his Tevas off his feet and on the bottom of the canoe, and now they were gone. He was disappointed, but I counted it as a blessing in disguise. He had been portaging in them as well and they had caused massive blisters on his feet. Now he would be forced to buy some real sneakers or boots in town which would protect his feet better. The Tevas simply weren't meant for miles of walking over uneven ground and trails.

About a mile north of the Saranac River outlet was a beach and public park. We pulled up in the sand and unloaded our gear, promptly getting everything covered in the fine white sand since it was soaking wet from our recent spill. The rain, which had been threatening all day, finally arrived. The day was not ending well. Just as we finished, Elizabeth pulled into the parking lot. We had called her the night before and again as we portaged around the last dam to make the arrangements.

"Hey darling. Good to see you!" I went in for a hug and kiss, but she pushed me away, wrinkling her nose and grinning.

"Eww. You stink. Stay away. Andy, come here, you can give me a hug instead. I'm sure you've been taking better care of yourself than Sam has." But I managed to get my hug in too, and my spirits immediately improved.

A quick fifteen minute drive and we were at her house with a hot shower, warm, dry clothes, couches, heating, a roof (good thing because it was absolutely pouring outside), and most importantly, food. We ate like kings, with barbeque chicken, potatoes, and fresh salad on the menu. One of the things you miss most while on a trail is fresh food, and the chance to eat green lettuce, carrots, tomatoes, etc. is not to be passed up lightly. Calories are of course important, but oh that delicious taste of greens!

Several beers later and Andy and I were dozing in our seats. Tough to stay awake after all the rapids and portaging we'd been doing. We fell asleep between clean, white, cotton sheets, dreaming of fairies and sugarplums.

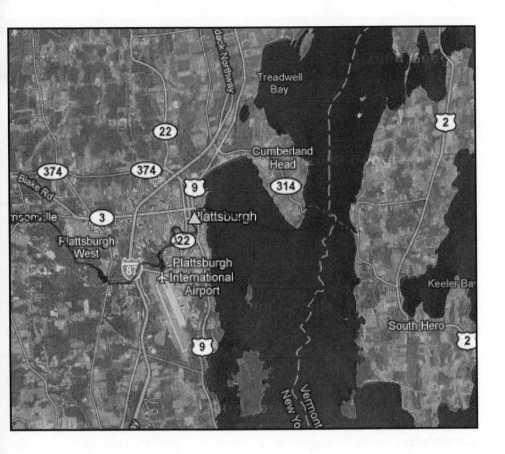

June 12th, Day 8 – Rest day near Plattsburgh: One look outside this morning and I had to do next-to-no work to convince Andy to take a zero day. With my girlfriend here, I of course was happy to stay put, and Andy was in no mood to paddle in the rain, so we decided to take our first day off.

'Zero days' – where no progress is made along a trail - hold a sacred place in my heart. On any trip they are an integral part of the itinerary. A day to recoup, regroup, and get some R & R is necessary for morale, gear, and overall health. Sore muscles get a chance to stretch out; gear gets a chance to be repaired and dried; and morale a chance to improve. We were in need of all three, so in spite of the added benefits of a beautiful lady to spend it with, and a great house at no cost to us, it allowed us to gain a better perspective on the trip.

We spread our tents, tarps, clothes, maps, etc. out in the garage. Much of it was soaking, and everything else could use the airing out anyways. Seven days of sweat and grime had done little for our overall odor. The wannigans were upended and more nails added to their base and handles. I tried to fashion a fastener for the lid to ensure a tighter fit, but did not discover an easy way to achieve one, so just left it with a, 'It's close enough.' Famous last words - I would eat them later on in Maine.

We drove back to Plattsburgh, stopping at the grocery store and the outdoor store to re-supply, and making a quick stop at a local farm stand for donuts, a weakness of mine. I promptly ate eight in the car, and finished the rest soon after we got back to the house.

The afternoon was spent languidly. We read, watched a movie (*Mr. and Mrs. Smith* – one of my favorite films) and played horseshoes, since the weather began to clear.

"Andy, what are you going to do next year? I mean, one year from now, we're hopefully going to be graduated and on our own. What's your plan?"

"I don't know. I think I'd like to work for the State Department. I think it would be really fascinating to work on foreign policy, and do some classified stuff. Probably not any James Bond work, but hopefully I'd get to work on some important, confidential projects. You?"

"I don't know either. I know I need to be outside. I love paddling and hiking around, and I love what we're doing now. But I'm not too sure how one might get paid to do it, you know?"

Andy laughed, "Yup, I know. It's tough to find people to pay you to have fun. Maybe you could write about it, you know, like a travel memoir or something?"

"Eh, maybe. I'm not a great writer. And besides, I think that that would take forever. We've done a lot of stuff already, and it's only been a week."

"Don't you want to do something that has meaning and that is important? I mean, like, canoeing is all well and good, but it doesn't really help anyone, right?"

I tossed my horseshoe, missing by a mile and digging up a big chunk of lawn. "Yes, but that doesn't really bother me. I think you've got to do what you want to do, and not worry about anyone else. No matter what. I mean, when it all comes down to it, we are this tiny insignificant living thing on a tiny planet in the middle of nowhere in a massive solar system. What we do isn't that important in the big scheme of things. So you might as well do what you enjoy."

Andy shook his head, "Well that's a hell of a way to look at things. You're depressing, you know that?"

I laughed. "No, it's not. You just said what everyone says when I tell them that, but for me, it cheers me up. To know that no matter what I do, it doesn't matter. That any action I take is meaningless. It means I should just do what I want to do, and not worry about anything else. Some people could take it too far if they don't have morals and be a little more Machiavellian with the philosophy, but not me. I'm a pretty good guy, so I'm not going to go out and steal something because it doesn't matter. To me, it just means that I should live my life the way I want to and not worry about others. If that means I want to help others out, great. If not, great too. But to me it means that I can do whatever I want and listen only to myself, to my heart, and not to what someone tells me."

"I guess. As long as that is what you get out of it, though I'm not sure how you managed it. But now you're stuck on how to make a living doing what you want to do, huh?"

"Yup. But I'll figure out some way. I'm not worried about it."

Andy won the horseshoes match by a hair, and we went inside to avoid the mosquitoes as dusk fell.

Dinner was ample amounts of steak and salmon and we went to bed well-rested, well-fed, and ready to be back on the water again. My frustration of the afternoon before had disappeared, and I was ready to begin the trip once more. Zero days are a godsend, and although too many can lead to a loss of purpose and frustration of a different kind, they should be used when needed, and this one was certainly necessary for our good spirits and continued enjoyment of the trip. Northern Forest Canoe Trail, here we come

Chapter 3: Lake Champlain

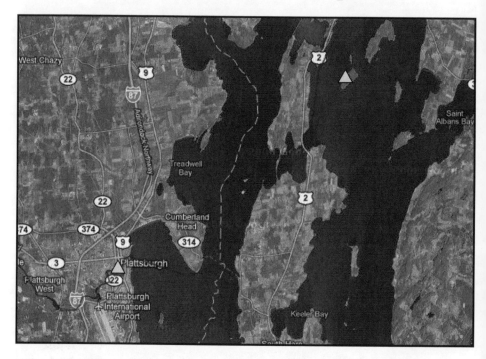

June 13th, Day 9 – Plattsburgh to Knight Island on Lake Champlain, Vermont: We woke up bright and early, but took our time with breakfast, and arrived at the lake where we had taken out two days previously at 10 o'clock. We met a woman at the dock who was monitoring for invasive species.

"Hey y'all. How're you doing?"

"Just fine. Just fine." We began to untie the canoe from the roof rack of Elizabeth's car.

"I'm a volunteer for the Lake Champlain Invasive Species Monitoring Program, and I was hoping I could ask you guys a couple questions about your canoe?"

Elizabeth looked at me and was about to tell a white lie about how our canoe has only been and will only be in Lake Champlain – she's a local and has dealt with these folks before – but I chimed in and told the woman that we had just traveled from Old Forge by water for the last week.

"…and then we traveled down the Saranac, arriving here the day before last. We took out right here so our boat has already been in Lake Champlain."

"That's fine. Where were you coming from again?" she repeated.

"Well we started in Old Forge on the Fulton Chain of Lakes, but we paddled here from there, and were in the lake two days ago. This boat came down the Saranac, so anything that was on the boat has already been in the lake."

"Has this boat been out in the sun for at least forty-eight hours since it was last used?"

"Well no, not quite." I was starting to get a little frustrated. "But you see, we paddled there from here, so anything that was on the boat is already in the waters here. You see?"

She seemed to ignore us. "You know, you should at least make sure the boat has a thorough chance to dry out, and you should remove any debris or leftover leaves, or algae or anything. Lake Champlain is a fragile ecosystem, and any little thing can throw it off. We have been fairly successful so far with our monitoring but we need continued vigilance in order to…"

I gave up trying to tell her that we were last in Lake Champlain, and that it didn't matter, and let Andy deal with her while I finished untying the boat and put it in the water. She just didn't seem to get it, and Andy had more patience than I did.

Invasive species are indeed a danger to lake ecosystems. She was correct in saying so, and with the vast majority of boaters she would meet it would be proper to try and get them to clean, drain and dry their boats. Invasive species can easily move across waterbodies and watersheds with the aid of an uncleaned boat. But for some reason she would not recognize that we were not changing water bodies or watersheds but were in fact returning to the same one. It just wasn't logical nor helpful for us to bother taking the steps to clean our boat – any invasives on it had come from the lake we were about to put into.

We finally managed to shove off, however, and paddled into fierce headwinds to round Cumberland Head. On Champlain at last! Lake Champlain is actually just a small remnant of what was once a much larger lake called Lake Vermont. It was 500 feet above the current level of Lake Champlain, and was formed during the last ice age from melting glaciers. Later on it became a salt water bay, part of the Atlantic Ocean, before waters receded, and it gradually dropped to its current level. Much of the lower Saranac and Mississquoi would have been under Lake Vermont, and we would have spent more than two days on lake had water levels remained as they were. We certainly would not have been able to where we did last night on the shore of today's Lake Champlain (Northern Forest Canoe Trail 2005)!

Fortunately waters did recede, and in 1609 Samuel de Champlain became the first European to see the lake. He, like most explorers, was exceedingly humble and unassuming, so he promptly named the lake for himself. He also managed to create a future 150 years of fighting between the French and

Iroquois by promptly killing two of their chiefs on this same journey (Northern Forest Canoe Trail 2005).

We, however, were simply paddling through, and hugged the shore in attempt to avoid the worst of the headwinds. We passed the MacDonough Monument at the mouth of the Saranac, commemorating Captain MacDonough's underdog naval victory against the British during the War of 1812. In the face of great odds, Captain MacDonough stood fast and went cannon-shot for cannon-shot with the British commander, aiming and firing the first cannon shot to score a hit himself. Through better maneuvering he was able to conquer the stronger force, though he was knocked down by falling debris, and thrown clear across his ship by the force of a well-aimed shot. By beating the British squadron, MacDonough was able to regain control of Lake Champlain, forcing the British army to retreat as well. And by forcing the British off Lake Champlain, the United States gained important leverage at the Treaty of Ghent, signed later that year. The Treaty's stipulations were much more favorable to the young United States than they might otherwise have been (Headley 1853).

This was not the only battle Lake Champlain has seen. Valcour Island, just to the south, was the site of one of Benedict Arnold's most important victories during the Revolutionary War, though it is not well known today. The British navy, led by Guy Carleton, had constructed a large fleet of ships on the northern shores of Lake Champlain, with the intention of sailing south to split the rebelling colonies in two, by controlling the Hudson River and Lake Champlain. Benedict Arnold, leading a ragtag ensemble of men with only eighteen small and under-armed ships, managed to thwart the British, and slow them enough to halt the campaign, and force them to retreat northwards again for the winter, thus ruining their plan for 1776 (Sellers 1930). The Americans took advantage of the extra time given them by Benedict Arnold, fortifying their forts and gearing up for the coming spring. When the British again attacked south in 1777, under 'Gentleman John' Burgoyne, the Americans were better prepared, and defeated the British soundly at the Battle of Saratoga, just west of the lake. The British had planned a three-pronged attack through New York to split the colonies in two and subdue the rebels. However, one prong was repelled at the Battle of Oriskany on August 3rd (Elizabeth and I passed a historical marker for it on the drive to Old Forge). The second prong never materialized when General William Howe attacked Philadelphia instead of moving north up the Hudson River. And the third prong was halted at Saratoga on October 7th. Benedict Arnold performed admirably at Saratoga as well, rallying the troops, and leading them on a death-defying charge to take the British position. The failure to recognize his actions at these two battles at least partially contributed to his turning traitor later in the war (Sellers 1930).

We finally managed to get around the point, after shipping some water from the high waves, and then flew down the lake with southerly winds at our back. We avoided the Plattsburgh ferry as it steamed by before paddling between

South Hero and North Hero Island. It was a beautiful day and there were motorboats, sailboats, and fishermen out by the dozen, all moving a lot faster than we were. Some of the boats made sizeable wakes, and they weren't always considerate enough to slow down when passing us, so we were subjected to some serious rolling.

A drawbridge separates the two Hero Islands, and we stopped for lunch while watching the boats queue up to await the opening of the bridge. We paddled up the east shore of North Hero island, and stopped in the hamlet of North Hero.

The Heroes were originally named "Great Island" by the Abenaki, but Ethan and Ira Allen renamed them North and South Hero in 1779. These islands were given to the Green Mountain Boys as grants to thank them for their service in stopping New York's claims to the land that is now Vermont (Northern Forest Canoe Trail 2005).

Vermont was originally part of New Hampshire, but land squabbles between New York and New Hampshire led to a ruling by King George III re-determining the border between the two states. The original settlers were told to get off their land since their old grants were now invalidated. In 1770, the New York government sent a sheriff to enforce the new ruling. The Green Mountain Boys were created to protect the land rights of these original settlers, and in 1777 they declared themselves the independent republic of Vermont. Things may have come to a head since neither New York, New Hampshire, Great Britain nor the itself-newly-created United States recognized the tiny republic, but the just-begun Revolutionary War took precedence (www.HistoricVermont.org 2010).

The Green Mountain Boys became involved in the Revolutionary War as well. Ethan Allen and Benedict Arnold led a party of Vermonters and other volunteers, taking Fort Ticonderoga - on the shores of Lake Champlain – from the British without firing a shot in 1775. The guns captured here were instrumental in forcing the British to leave Boston the following summer. They also participated in the Battle of Bennington, a side battle to Burgoyne's southern thrust in 1777, which denied him badly-needed supplies by routing a strong force of British and Hessian mercenaries (Lonergan 1974).

Vermont remained a separate entity after the war, and Ethan Allen almost became a traitor himself when he threatened to turn Vermont over to Canada, since Congress refused to recognize Vermont as a state. Fortunately, Congress changed their mind, and Vermont was recognized as the fourteenth state in 1791 (The Ethan Allen Homestead Museum 2010).

There was little in North Hero except for a general store, but what a general store it was. Several floors of touristy knick-knacks were packed into a rambling farmhouse, which also included groceries, a deli, and a small bookstore. We wandered around, trying on hats, and munching on ice cream cones. The deli's sandwiches were named for historical figures of the area, so they included Samuel de Champlain, Ethan and Ira Allen, and even a Benedict Arnold (not a specified sandwich, the Benedict Arnold was instead a 'make-up-your-own-sandwich-if-you-can't-decide-on-any-of-the-others', a reference to his traitorous ways).

We wandered up and down Main Street, but failed to find anything else of interest, so hopped back in our boat and paddled across to Knight Island, arriving there nice and early in the afternoon. The campsite on the northern point was open and we set up our tents and the tarp on the gravel tip extending out into the water. We cooled off with a swim, and spent the afternoon reading and exploring the island (not much to speak of, except for a number of other campsites) under the hot afternoon sun. I kicked Andy's butt in checkers, and we ate a delicious dinner of hot dogs and chili, before watching a magnificent sunset over the Adirondacks to the west. To think we were in the heart of them just a short week ago.

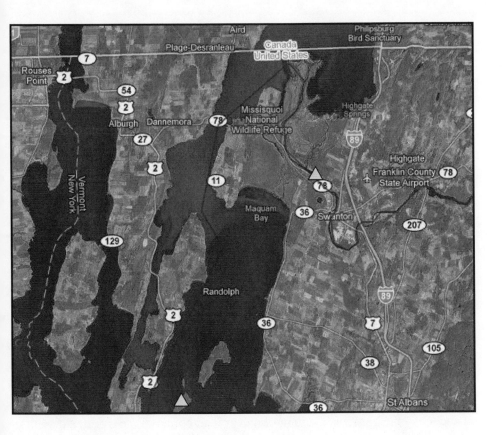

June 14th, Day 10 – Knight Island to the Mississquoi River near Swanton:
Bright blue skies and a hot sun greeted us this morning. A slight breeze from the
south also boded well for our northward paddle.

Lakes, especially large lakes like Champlain, often result in rather
boring, repetitive paddling. When out in the middle of the lake, it can feel like no
progress is being made, and with little change in the scenery, it is quite easy to
drift off into reverie. Andy and I would paddle for hours without saying anything,
each drifting in and out of our own thoughts. Then something would pique our
interest.

"Andy, what do you know about the Great Wall?" Maybe it was a stone
wall along the shore, or that was simply the direction my thoughts had headed.
Often, neither of us knew anything and we might hypothesize about its origins.

It could be a light-hearted conversation such as, "Sam, would you rather
be a giraffe or a baboon?" (Giraffe, of course. I am 6'4" after all.) Or it could
take a much more serious in tone such as, "What do you think about re-
incarnation?"

Some question would come to mind, and we would chat for the next hour
on any number of diverse topics, from the Irish potato famine to the schedule of

our school rugby team next season to just how big ostrich eggs actually are. We had all the time in the world, and we would discuss topics at length, occasionally arguing, but often just chatting. It helped time pass, and I certainly learned a thing or two about, well, a lot of things.

On the water we quickly passed Gull Island, marked on the map but in reality little more than a large rock jutting out from the water. No gulls in sight. We stopped briefly on the northern tip of North Hero Island to refill our water bottles and use the facilities.

The beach next to where we landed was roped off to protect the nesting grounds of the threatened spiny soft-shell turtle. We saw several throughout the afternoon, basking in the sun. They were certainly doing better than we were. By the time the afternoon rolled around, I felt as though my brains were beginning to fry. The combination of no cover, little breeze, and a cloudless sky resulted in an oven-like quality to the lake. Not only were we exposed to the direct sunlight, but the lake acted as a mirror and reflected much of the heat back, doubling the agony. Our tans were quickly becoming burns.

We passed under the Mississquoi Bay Bridge, and then paddled to the Mississquoi River delta, within a quarter mile of the Canadian border.

Since Lake Champlain straddles the Canadian border, and has dozens of island and inlets, it has been a highway for smugglers ever since the profession became lucrative here. During Prohibition, Lake Champlain enjoyed a brief but lurid period of midnight boat trips, frantic winter car chases across its frozen expanses, and occasional gunfights. Fortunately the "Dirty Thirties" are behind us and today the border is the longest unpatrolled border in the world, although the burgeoning drug trade may change that eventually.

Leaving Lake Champlain behind (and also any chance of sighting Champ, the resident lake monster, supposedly of similar origin as the Loch Ness monster), we began our first paddle upstream of the trip. We ate lunch just after entering the river, and watched a woman reel in brown trout after brown trout. She cast shoddily, got her line tangled several times, and was clearly a newcomer to fishing, but she managed to catch four or five while we sat and watched. He husband sat next to her, glowering, as his line lay limp in the water. Beginner's luck I suppose, but it probably helped that the river had been stocked just the week or two before.

It was also at lunch that the 'tire game' was born. The Mississquoi River flows through miles of Vermont farmland, so pollution, such as fertilizers and field runoff, is a problem. We had been told to carry water from towns to drink, and not to trust the river water, even if we filtered it. It also meant that there was some solid waste in the rivers, everything from beach chairs to fenders, and most certainly tires. Since we spotted several from our vantage point as we munched on peanut butter and jelly, a game was born. Quite simple, a tire spotted in the water equals a point for the spotter. It began incongruously enough, but soon grew all out of proportion, especially later on, on the Clyde River.

We bush-camped in a fern grove along the side of the river, with a house visible through the woods about 200 yards away, and the road clearly in sight on the other side of the river. Unfortunately, we didn't have a lot of options, but the ferns turned out to be surprisingly nice. We knocked down just enough to set up our tents and created a space for the fire and our gear, and it resulted in a sort of fort, a little snug nest in among the waist high ferns. If you knelt down (and plugged your ears) you could even pretend that civilization was far, far away, instead of far too close.

Chapter 4: The Mississquoi River

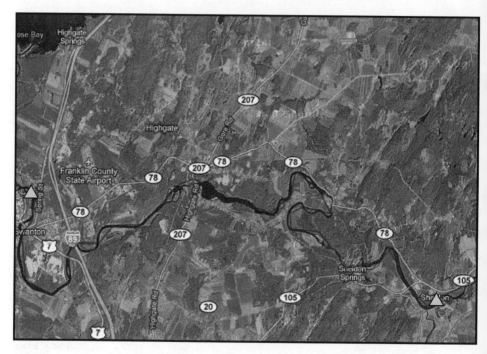

June 15th, Day 11 – Mississquoi River to Mississquoi River near Sheldon Junction: We skipped breakfast this morning again, and paddled several miles upstream to arrive in Swanton, Vermont. The diner in town was closed on Mondays (whoever heard of that?!) so we walked about a mile to another one and ate a delicious breakfast anyways. It's tough to mess up pancakes and eggs, especially with the appetites we had.

After breakfast we walked up Main Street and stopped in at the Abenaki Tribal Museum. Two ladies were at the front desk of the Community Center, next door, and we asked to be let into the museum.

"Certainly." She didn't look at us twice. We hadn't shaved in days and our shirts had begun to stink worse than ever, but she was pleased to let us look around. We walked over to the door which she unlocked before turning on the lights.

"Bring the key back when you're done. And turn out the lights. If you have any questions, please ask. I'll be right next door."

"Thanks so much!"

This sort of treatment would never have occurred in a larger city, but in Swanton, when two strangers show up, looking disheveled and smelling worse, you let them have the keys to the place. The gesture made my day.

The museum was a small room, but well-lit and packed with Abenaki artifacts. Fishing rods and nets hung from nails, bows and spears were propped up in corners, and blankets and tapestries filled the walls. Life-sized mannequins demonstrated traditional every-day wear, wedding garments, battle attire, and ceremonial costumes. Plaques were posted beneath each artifact and piece of artwork, describing what it was, what it was made of, and its use or design. Full page printouts were also posted on the walls, describing much of Abenaki history, from pre-European arrival on through their history of fighting in the French and Indian War, the Revolutionary War, and the War of 1812, as well as the Vermont eugenics project (up to 200 people, including many Abenaki, were "voluntarily" sterilized under An Act for Human Betterment by Voluntary Sterilization passed in 1931), and their current struggle for recognition as a tribe in Vermont and the United States. They, like many Native American tribes, have endured persecution for hundreds of years, and still are not a nationally recognized tribe. Vermont recognized the Abenaki in 1976, but later withdrew recognition, and their application for national recognition is still pending. They have a rich history, and deserve the rights, benefits, and funding that the United States gives to other tribes.

We wandered around, calling quietly to each other as a particular tid-bit caught our attention.

"Andy, check out the war paint on this guy!"

"Sam, come here. Imagine trying to construct this spear without any iron tools." It was fascinating.

One plaque detailed their current efforts which include lobbying at the state and national levels, and non-violent protests such as bush-camping, and 'fish-ins' – similar to a sit-in except that instead of sitting against the law, the Abenaki fish against the law, asserting their traditional right to determine their own fishing laws.

The last plaque stated that (and I paraphrase), 'Abenaki fires can still be seen burning brightly along the riverbanks during summer evenings, proof that our spirit still glows strongly in the breast of many, and that the Abenaki tradition will continue.' We were proud to be emulating that tradition, and adding to the firelight along the river, our one blaze a small contribution to an important part of Native American history.

Continuing on up the river, we dodged left and right across the river, staying in eddies as often as possible, and simply hugging the bank when not. Paddling upstream is a lot more challenging than downstream, not only because the current is going against you, but also because you need to constantly be reading the river so that you can take advantage of any eddy or swirl in the current. If the current is swifter at one section, then you dig in and paddle as quickly as possible, trying to crest over the rim and beat the river. You can feel yourself move uphill in some spots, particularly if you are in the stern, and you can watch the bow rise up an inch or two as you paddle furiously to top out over the rise and move upstream. Sometimes only inches are gained at a time, and sometimes, you literally don't move. It can be frustrating, excruciatingly frustrating at times, especially towards the end of the day, but also, like all paddling, it can be extremely satisfying, as you conquer the river little by little.

We portaged around several dams, including one of the inflatable variety. A huge rubber tube stretched across the top of the concrete base, stapled into the concrete. It looked like a long inner tube on steroids. It must have been extremely thick to withstand the pressure behind it.

Late afternoon rolled around and we paddled past the site of a former covered bridge. I read my map, and then did a double take. It stated that Confederate soldiers had raided here and tried to burn the bridge! I had always thought that the Confederates never made it north of Gettysburg, but apparently they managed to. These particular soldiers raided south from Canada, robbing and looting St. Albans, Vermont on October 19th, 1864. They made off with about $220,000 worth of bank bonds and cash before attempting to set fire to the town (and failing) and racing north towards Canada. Local citizens gave chase so the Confederate raiders attempted to burn the bridge, but this fire was quickly put out by the pursuers as well. They did manage to cross into Canada but 14 of the 21 were promptly arrested, and $90,000 was restored to St. Albans. The remaining seven made good on their escape (Kinchen 1970; Northern Forest Canoe Trail 2005).

We didn't get to camp until 6:30 after a very long day on the river. We even managed to find headwinds on the river, in addition to the current we were already battling. But we made it to one of the few official campsites on this section, and were presently surprised to find that the Lussier family who caretakes the site had provided it with firewood already. It was a huge blessing for us, since we were just about out of energy and we praised the Lussiers as we unpacked. We put the tarp up and quickly set up our tents before settling down to an entirely unsatisfying dinner of freeze-dried Asian food. We ate it anyways, and pronounced it fit for kings, before turning in almost immediately afterwards, but not before watching a strange man wander through the woods nearby. There were no signs of houses, so we hoped he was a Lussier...

June 16th, Day 12 – Mississquoi River to Mississquoi River near East Berkshire: The day dawned bright and sunny and I woke early, raring to go and do some serious upstream rapids. One mile of Class II rapids ended right at our campsite, so the first order of business for the day was to get up these. I decided that today was the day when I would start poling, so I chopped down a smallish pine, limbed it and was ready to go. It was perhaps slightly too large, and certainly much heavier than it should have been since it was still green wood and full of liquid, but I determined it would do. Andy could only look dubiously on. We loaded the boat and were off. I poled successfully for the first fifteen minutes, navigating through rocks and dodging from eddy to eddy, resting a minute behind a rock before nudging the bow out into the current and pushing forcefully upwards to get into the next eddy, and doing it all over again. Andy helped by paddling as I pushed, and by pulling and pushing off rocks in the bow.

My movements were jerky from little practice (I hadn't poled in years) and the current was moving quickly. I kept up a running commentary of "Okay, now edging out around this rock…Now! Paddle!…okay now duck in behind this rock…good…good" and so on. Andy, game as always, worked strenuously to help my poor attempts and we moved little by little upstream.

These Class II rapids however, were a bit out of my poling league, and sure enough, as I nudged the bow out again from behind a rock, perhaps 800 yards into the rapids, I lost my grip on the pole and let the bow begin to turn downstream, which meant the boat turned perpendicular to the stream, facing the left bank. The downstream gunwale clipped a rock and over we went. Fortunately, the river was fairly shallow and the boat was pressed up against the rock we had just clipped, so the gear went nowhere. We took it all out and balanced it precariously on rocks poking upwards out of the water, emptied the boat, and reloaded, finding we had lost only our bailer which had somehow come untied from the stern handle (and the pole, which I purposely let drift away in my frustration). No more poling from now on, we would stick to lining which, while more painful with stubbed toes and banged shins, and certainly less graceful, would at least be safer. I *hate* to flip.

We finished the set by lining, not a terrible prospect on a hot day. The bow is the easier position while lining, since you can see the ground in front of you (if it is visible through the rushing water) for better footing, while at the stern the boat covers the riverbed you are walking up, forcing you to stumble along blindly. The preferred technique is to lean with most of your weight on the bow deck of the boat, gliding upstream by jumping and skipping from rock to rock. The bow is much steadier and more reliable as a balance aid than the rocky riverbed, and leaning heavily on the canoe prevents many an otherwise painful and wet fall - an occurrence often unavoidable in the stern.

We continued our paddle upstream, stopping in Enosburg Falls for lunch at Subway, and to view the Bridge of Flowers and Light, a pedestrian bridge that crosses the river over the dam in town. Clearly some hippies were in charge of the naming committee on this one.

The afternoon was spent paddling (surprise) upstream, but we were in no particular hurry, and we took our time. The current moved quickly in some spots, but in most cases we were able to overcome it and by paddling hard and digging deep we remained in the canoe for much of the time. We were forced to line a breached dam, dodging not only rocks but exposed Rebar, remnants from an earlier time when a butter churn factory existed on the riverbank. Andy had a near call when he slipped and caught himself just in front of some Rebar, and I ended up in some water too deep to stand and had to have Andy rescue me by pulling the canoe towards him, but we made it without any undue events.

We passed a massive snapping turtle out sunning himself before stopping quickly in East Berkshire where we bought a couple of cold Cokes, and I got a new baseball cap (NASCAR since they had no other logos). We also refilled our water bottles for the night, since the river is still too dirty to be drinking from. We have been passing working farms all day, and the stink from the manure and machinery has sometimes been almost overpowering. The 'tire game' was still going at full tilt, and Andy was winning 8-7. The way the river looked today, however, the game could have been played with a number of different types of waste and the score would still have grown. Not the world's cleanest river.

We had planned to camp at Doe campsite, another campsite on private land run by a family, but when we arrived at the bend in the river where it was marked to be, we saw only a soaring riverbank bluff, 60-70 feet high of steep, eroded, sand.

These banks, incidentally, tell the history of the river's rise and fall over time, and there have been some doozies. In 1927 two small storms stalled over the area and dumped a record rainfall over an already sodden area, causing the Flood of 1927 which is the region's most devastating natural disaster. Houses, barns, and even a hydroelectric plant were swept downstream, and hundreds of acres of farmland abutting the river were destroyed. Vermonters responded with their typical obstinacy and indomitable spirit, and rebuilt along the river, even towing a house and barn back up the river on ice the following winter to its original spot.

We consulted the map, looked again, and then got out of the boat and scrambled to the top, slipping and sliding the whole way as the sand gave way easily beneath our steps. At the top was indeed an old picnic table, a fire ring, and some tent sites, but after struggling to make it up with only the clothes on our backs, we decided the effort involved in trying to bring our gear up was not worth it, so we descended via leaps and bounds back to the river edge, our sneakers now full of sand. Across the river was a much more manageable bank, only 7 feet high with a flat plateau of ferns above it, and we crossed to camp there. Another beautiful fern campsite and I couldn't have been happier. We hollowed out our nook in the chest high plants and cooked freeze-dried BBQ Chicken mixed in with rice, potatoes, corn, and Ramen. Cleaned out the wannigan, so time to resupply tomorrow.

We sat by the river afterwards, looking for otters or weasels, or anything, but saw only water, flowing irrevocably onwards. Andy and I didn't say anything, instead simply sitting with our legs hanging off the bank over the water, content with each others' silent company. The last rays of sunlight shafted through the trees, creating a collage of bars of light and dark around us. Pastels were painted across the sky over nearby fields, and we were far enough away from roads that no cars roared in the distance.

Out here, on the river, life – real life that is – seems so far away. We have escaped, however temporarily, the hustle and bustle of school, work, family, and all the other responsibilities and requirements that weigh us down. Instead, we get to really *live*. The glide of the canoe, the chirp of the bird, the music of the wind brushing the fern fronds against each other are all subtly magical in their own individual way. I rested my head back against a fern tussock, looked at the night sky peering through the branches overhead and sighed the deep sigh of a contented man. Andy too would look up from his righting to simply peer across the slow moving water, absorbing with all his being this peaceful night. Night fell and as we crawled into our sleeping bags, the only sound that lulled us to sleep was that of crickets.

June 17th, Day 13 – Mississquoi River to Mississquoi River near Glen Sutton, Quebec: We slept in perhaps an hour, the intoxication from the previous evening's sunset no doubt prolonging our dreams, and didn't get on the river until a few minutes to nine. Several hours on the river got us to Richford, Vermont, doing some tough miles which were predominantly lining. It was frustrating, but we inched onwards. The town had a boom in the early '20s, but has seen a downward spiral ever since, which was pretty clear as we walked through it. Broken-down and despondent old men smoked on door steps, with little to do except loaf, and dirty children played in the street. We received the evil eye from almost everyone and gained not even a nod of recognition or greeting as we portaged through town up the main street. Paint was scattered on the side walk and the houses looked ready to crumble, a smell of decay wafting nearby. We stopped quickly in the grocery store to pick up supplies, but saw no need to dawdle and got back on the river quickly.

The afternoon was much more pleasant, and saw us paddle up a gentle current all the way to the Canadian border. We pulled over to the right –

American – bank and climbed to the bridge that crossed the river and the border, explaining our trip to the customs officers.

"Well that sure is something. You fellas sure have set out on a journey. But you don't need to check in with us since you're leaving here, not coming here. You know what, let me check your info here anyways, just in case."

In case of what, I didn't ask.

"You haven't been arrested for anything have you?"

"Nope."

"You carrying any fresh fruits or vegetables?"

"Nope."

"The Canadians shouldn't give you any troubles at all, so don't worry." We weren't. "How long are you going to be in Canada?"

"We're not sure. Three or four days about. Perhaps five. It depends on how fast we move, the weather, et cetera."

"And you're sure you're not carrying any produce, or fireworks or anything?"

"Of course not." We could have been smuggling nuclear warheads and twelve small children, but they would have had no idea, since no one, American or Canadian, went down and checked the boat.

"Well don't you worry about anything. The Canadians are no trouble at all." We still weren't, and were starting to be anxious about getting on our way, since this check-in did not matter and was not required. Finally, after several more of the same questions, phrased in different ways, they sent us on our way promising that they would radio the Canadian border that we were coming.

We walked across the bridge and up the hill to the Canadian customs office, and the officer walked out to greet us. She took our passports, and when we started to say who we were and what we were doing, she cut us off with a heavily accented, "I know, they radioed."

We stood silently while she quickly examined our passport before asking, "Any vegetables or booze?"

Our headshake "no" was enough to reassure her, and she handed back our passports and with a quick, "Good luck," she returned to her office. Obviously the Americans need to take a page from the Canadians' book, since the Canadians are a model of efficiency.

We walked back across the bridge, and as we approached the other side of the river, a new officer who had just pulled in in his pick-up announced to the office "Two pedestrians on the bridge!"

We reached the other side of the bridge and hopped the guardrail to return down to the river and our boat, when the new officer, suddenly looking frantic and reaching for his hip, barked out, "Hey! Wait! Stop!" We froze, but one of the officers we had first talked to rushed out and calmed down the irate new guy. Clearly it was the most excitement they had had in weeks.

Although the border is quite calm these days, smuggling was a profitable enterprise for both Canadians and Americans in recent history. The Canadians smuggled alcohol from Vermont in 1918-19 when Prohibition was in effect there, and the trade was reversed from 1920 to 1933 when the United States became dry. The goods crossing the border slowed to a trickle when those acts were repealed, and today the drug trade is what predominantly concerns the border patrol. While never on the same scale as on the Mexican border, it has been increasing in recent years, and officials are increasingly watchful. It is only a matter of time before crossing becomes more stringent, as evidenced by the recent change from only a driver's license needed to a full-fledged passport required to make the border crossing. As other entry points disappear, drug smugglers will drift to the relatively unnoticed Canadian border as a way to get their product into the United States, and once that occurs, more attention will be paid. Supply and demand is a beautiful thing.

We paddled several miles past the border, and made camp along the left bank, only a few hundred yards from a road and houses. Our options were limited, and though there were some low bushy trees to conceal us, the ground was lumpy and swampy, and there was little of the beauty and peace of the previous night. Trucks roared past as we made dinner of hot dogs and beans. Let's be frank (of course no pun here), hot dogs and beans can improve any situation.

June 18th, Day 14 – Mississquoi River to North Branch Mississquoi River near Mansonville: We woke up to discover we had had some surprise nocturnal visitors. Our tents, wannigans, and gear were covered in slugs, and we were forced to spend an extra twenty minutes to flick them off our stuff. Andy got me with a big juicy one, right across the back, that he was especially aggressive about flicking from his gear. I suppose it serves us right for camping in a swamp.

The morning was very uneventful. We paddled upstream against a steady but not overpowering current, exiting the boat only twice. It was pleasant to be paddling more often than lining instead of vice versa like the previous morning. We reached the split of the Mississquoi under darkening skies and ate lunch under a bridge as the first raindrops began to fall. Now on the North Branch of the Mississquoi, we paddled on a much narrower stream, though it was still deep enough to get a full paddle length in. At one point we were lost in reverie as we continued on, when suddenly, 'Snap!' one of the four bolts holding the bow seat to the gunwales broke and Andy tumbled backwards onto the gear. I just laughed while Andy looked rueful, grumbling about shoddy quality.

I told him, "Andy, lose the pounds," but he just shook his head and grimaced at me.

"You'll be next," he prophesied, and he would be right.

We quickly pulled over and repaired the break with a piece of spare string in its place, but this would spell the beginning of the end for the seat. We portaged through Mansonville .7 miles, the only portage of the day, then changed into our cleanest clothes and prepared to spend the afternoon in town.

First stop was the grocery store (épicerié) before it closed. In the checkout line we discovered it cost 5 cents per every bag you used, an effort at reducing plastic consumption. It seemed to be effective since almost everyone there used their own bags. The States would do well to follow their lead. We dropped the food back at the gear and boat, then went to the library (bibliotheque) and checked my email, the standing of the Red Sox, etc. The hardware store (droguerie) did not have any bolts long enough to replace our broken one, so the string will have to do for now.

We browsed through town afterwards, doing some window shopping and reading the historical markers on the green, in front of the church (église), and at the fire station (caserne de pompiers). Our jaws dropped temporarily at the price of gas - $1.05 9/10 – before realizing that that was per liter, not per gallon. Nothing really piqued our interest, however, so we stepped into the bar (bar!) even though it was only 3 o'clock.

Several locals had beaten us, and the bartender was of course holding forth. We joined right in, buying a pair of Labatt's. The bartender appeared to be in her low twenties, about our age, and since she was cute we immediately began a conversation. She of course asked our purpose in town, so we told her and the other men what we were doing. Everyone was suitably impressed, and they said that a kayaker had been through a couple of weeks before on the same trail, one of the guys we'd been hearing about.

Talk drifted on, and we learned how the fishing season had been going.

"You know, they stock the river every year, eh? And they stock it just right south of town here, you know, eh? So we go out and fish it right after they've done stocking it, and it's pretty good, you know eh? Especially if it's raining like it's doing now, eh?"

Well, we knew it had been raining. We had been camping in it for the past couple weeks. Eh?

The beer kept coming and we ended up getting into an argument over the relative merits of full-contact broomball. Andy especially was a proponent.

"We play broomball at school in Maine, but there isn't any contact. I think you've got it right there. Full-contact would be a great idea. Then we could really lay 'em out. Sam and I are pretty good ourselves, and we're big guys, so we could really do some damage."

The fisherman got really into it, demonstrating enthusiastically his imagined checking technique, punctuated by "Like this, eh?" and "Right there, you know?" I know I wouldn't have wanted to play him.

We stumbled out of there after what seemed like ages only to find that it was only six, and pouring rain in buckets. So much for our drinking capacity. We ate at the restaurant across the street, though what I'm not sure. A shingle would have tasted just fine in the state I was in, but fortunately I think whatever they fed us was at least edible. We made friends with the waitress and owner, since we were the only two there, as well as the cook. She offered us a place in her barn, which she said was only a couple of miles upstream, but knowing we could never paddle that far, we politely (I hope) declined. Then we drifted down to our canoe, sodden by the time we got there but not caring, before climbing in and paddling around the corner. We set up our tents in the still torrential downpours, and climbed in immediately. I promised Andy we would eat some chocolate for dessert in a minute, but I promptly passed out, and Andy was left to eat alone. The rain continued all night, but we were dead to the world, and it did not bother us one whit.

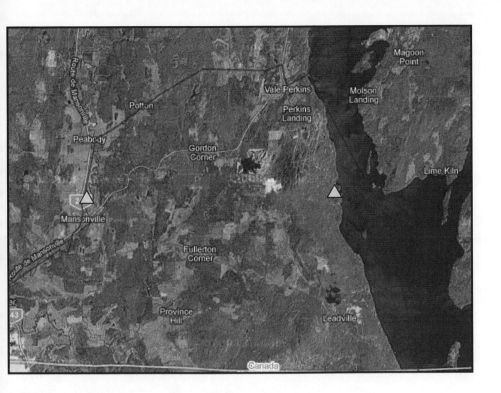

June 19th, Day 15 – North Branch Mississquoi River to Lake Memphremagog: I awoke to a headache and the drip, drip, drip of the rain still coming down. Fortunately my med-kit for the trip included Advil (actually, that is *all* it included) so I popped a few capsules and set about to build a fire, with Andy still snoring gently in his own tent. We had neglected to get firewood last night (not too surprising considering our state) so I scrounged around nearby and grabbed some damp wood, birch bark and some small twigs as well. Started with birch bark stripped into really small pieces, but it wouldn't light. Some smoke and a quick smolder on the very tip before it fizzled into nothing. It didn't help that the rain continued to fall onto my kindling. Next I tried knife shavings, then finally I tore some paper from my notebook, all to no avail. Anything that began dry quickly became sodden. I spent perhaps twenty minutes fiddling with the kindling before throwing in the towel and bringing out the little stove I had brought for emergency purposes. It of course flared up immediately, and I had breakfast in no time. Not that I was pleased. I pride myself on my woodcraft, and this failure (the only one of the trip, though we did have days upon days of rain later in Maine) nettled me.

We paddled several miles upstream against a gentle current, winding this way and that along the small stream, passing cow pasture and fences. It was actually quite peaceful, and since the river was deep we had no trouble getting a full paddle-length into the water. There is nothing more frustrating than trying to claw your way upstream against a current when the river is so shallow that you can't get in a full stroke.

Then we rounded a bend and ahead of us was the bridge that marked the takeout for the longest portage of the trip: the Grand Portage. It was an historic 5.7 mile portage frequented by the Abenaki people who knew it as a "Carrying Place." They were much brighter than we were and kept a canoe on either side, so all they had to do was carry themselves and perhaps their rifle across, retrieving their canoe on the other side from wherever they had hidden/sunk it (Northern Forest Canoe Trail 2005). We however, had to hump all our gear and the canoe across its length.

We took a minute to collect ourselves under the bridge after unloading. Then I stood up suddenly, and with an, "It ain't getting any shorter," I threw up the canoe and set off.

It turned out to be a breeze. It was all along a dirt road, and I marked in my head crossroads from the map at 1/3 of the way there, 2/3 of the way there, and 5/6 of the way there, breaking it up into more manageable chunks to wrap my head around, much the way one does with a seemingly impossible task. Just break it down into simple chunks you know you can do, and before you know it, it's over. My tump was perfect since I had adjusted it before setting out, and I just sang tunes in my head, and did a lot of thinking about everything from women to my plans following the trip's end. Several cars passed with canoes strapped to their roofs, their drivers clearly proud that they were bright enough to portage with cars. Little do they know that it's a lot more satisfying to carry it under your own power (at least that's what I keep telling myself.) Before I knew it, I had crested the height of land and was looking down on Lake Memphremagog, and a short distance later I was setting the canoe down on the boat launch. No problem, and I felt as though I could walk back with it again. (Not that I did, of course.)

I knocked on the door of the boat launch tender who was in his little shack, and with my bad French, and his bad English I managed to get him to wash the boat, a necessary chore when putting into Memphremagog. It was another attempt at preventing the spread of invasive species, and frankly the canoe needed the power wash so I didn't complain. While washing, he told me about the new stock of 3000 brown trout which, given the language barrier between us, demonstrated just how big the news was to the locals. The fact that he attempted pleasantries at all was amazing. Andy showed up a short time later, and we returned ½ mile down the road to a general store we had passed to get some drinks before heading back for the second load.

We plopped our weary bodies on the front bench with cold Cokes in our hand. The owner of the store, an older lady, came out and promptly began to chat. She was very forward and rather blunt as she told us about the store, the customers, the town, and her life.

"I've lived here for my whole life, but I've done a fair amount of traveling as well. I know this isn't much here, but it's home, you know? I know these people, I know how they work, and I like it here. Sure it may not be as busy as somewhere else, but it's nice."

"But what do you *do*?"

"Fish, talk, go to the movies a couple town over. Or just enjoy life. It's peaceful here."

Her candor made it all quite funny since she looked objectively at the whole town and store life she enjoyed, and she was a pleasure to talk to. There had also been several of the kayakers who were out in front of us at the store, and she told us they were still about a week or two in front, and she questioned the amount of gear we had, our wannigan utility, and the fact that we carried, not wheeled, the canoe.

"It'd be easier, you know? Those wooden boxes what-cha-ma-call-its just look painful. You should get some bags and some wheels, make it easier on yourselves."

We grinned and told her we were going the old-fashioned way, and she just rolled her eyes.

The second load posed little trouble as well, and we stopped again at the general store for a second round of drinks. By this time we had walked almost eighteen miles, and we were really worn out, so we spent at least an hour just sipping Coke and resting in the shade. The day had cleared to only clouds with the occasional hint of sunshine, and we were thankful for the rest. The owner came out and harassed us again, calling us lazy and useless. But she took our empty cans and even gave me back a quarter in return for the empty bottle deposits. I asked her the weather and since she didn't know, she insisted I come inside and watch the weather channel to find out. A nicer and friendlier lady couldn't be found on the Trail, and I hope she is repaid at some point for her kindness and generosity to us poor canoeists. We greatly appreciated her help.

Just as we were about to leave, our friend from the night before in the bar walked in. He was working a road construction job nearby and had stopped in for a drink. It was pleasant to say hello and feel like a local, knowing everyone who walked in the door.

We finally managed to get back down to the water and set off again, grateful to be under paddle power, instead of foot. Several miles along the shore was a campsite, unmarked on our maps but obviously of use for the needy paddler. We took advantage of it and ate a well-earned dinner of spaghetti before turning out the lights before the sun had set. Today, we went to bed with our feet, not our shoulders, sore, a first for the trip.

Chapter 5: The Clyde and Nulhegan Rivers

June 20th, Day 16 – Lake Memphremagog to the Clyde River near West Charleston, Vermont: We awoke to a foggy morning. I got up early as always in spite of the hard day we had yesterday, and made breakfast. I also replaced the slap-dash job I had done fixing the bow seat with some stronger string from my tent, reinforcing the spot where the bolt had broken.

By the time we got on the water the fog had burnt off slightly, but awesome cloud formations overshadowed us, some foreboding and others simply beautiful with their wind-torn formations whisping and whorling about. A slight drizzle followed us intermittently, but the clear sky we could see off to the east gradually overtook us and we had bluer skies for the afternoon. We threaded our way through dozens of fishermen out for the morning, chasing perhaps the newly stocked trout that had made it down to the lake somehow, or perhaps simply out enjoying the morning, foggy though it was.

We paddled the length of Memphremagog easily, hitting Newport around 11:30. We chuckled as we cross the border, about halfway down the lake, and saw a cleared slash through the forest on shore, perhaps 50 yards wide, corresponding with a slash that bisected an island to the east, demarcating the border. Memphremagog also saw its share of rumrunners, in both winter and summer, who used the lake with its many islands and coves to cross whiskey and other liquor to the forbidden side. In summer, boats would flit in and out of coves evading the patrols while in winter, cars would make a break for it across the frozen lake in winter. Recently, a diver found bottles intact with whiskey still inside on the lake bottom, relics of Prohibition (Northern Forest Canoe Trail 2005).

Memphremagog, like Champlain, was also involved in wartime. Robert Rogers, leader of Robert's Rangers, moved with a force of British soldiers up Lake Champlain against Saint-François, an Abenaki village. The French got wind of the attack before it occurred and guarded against their proposed return route back across Lake Champlain. Roger's Rangers instead were forced to make their escape along the shores of Lake Memphremagog. They subsequently crossed the Nulhegan River and eventually made it down the Connecticut to return to friendlier lands, though not before a number of the rangers were captured, killed and/or scalped (Ross 2009).

John Stark, the celebrated Revolutionary War general of whom more will be said later, also spent time on the lake involuntarily, when he was held for ransom after being spirited away from his home by Indians. His subsequent bravery under duress as their captive earned him respect. He was forced to run the gauntlet between two rows of paddle-wielding Indians. Stark instead grabbed a paddle from one and threatened to "kiss all of their women." Instead of provoking his captors, he inspired their admiration and his later protests at doing "squaw's work" further earned their respect. He later was ransomed and continued to guide parties in the region (Rose 2007).

The lake monster Memphre (probably a close relation of Champ) haunts the lake, but he must have slept in this morning since we saw no sign of him on our paddle. According to a plaque he was once sighted by dozens of passengers onboard the steamer *Anthemis* so there must be no doubt of his continued existence to this day. Ha.

Newport is a bustling Vermont town, but there is no customs office. A direct connection via phone to somewhere else appears to suffice, and we got out our passports, and then picked up the receiver. The conversation went something like this:

"Hi, my name is Sam Brakeley. We just arrived from Canada in a canoe"

"Um okay, hold on a minute, let me find the forms… (Let me remind you this is a direct connection to a customs office. The only reason I might call would be to check into the country. They should have the forms in front of them.)

"Ah yes, here they are. Let's see. Name, Sam Brakeley. What is the name of your boat and where is it registered?"

"Um, it's a canoe, it's not registered anywhere."

- 65 -

"Hmm, no registration huh? Well, what is the hull number?"

"It's just a canoe. It doesn't have a number."

"Is there a motor on it?"

"Nope, no motor. Just a canoe that we paddled."

"Hmmm...alright, I guess I'll just leave these blank..." (duh)

"You're sure there isn't a number?"

"Pretty darn sure sir"

"Well, okay. Where are you going?"

"To Fort Kent, Maine."

"Who is driving you there?"

"No one, we are canoeing to Maine."

"So how are you going to get there?"

"We are paddling."

"Right. So who is going to pick you up? Do you have a brother, or relative, or friend or something to pick you up and drive you?"

"Nope. We are paddling there in our canoe."

Unfortunately, the conversation didn't end there. It took several more minutes to finally get our point across and explain to him the Trail and what we were doing. But I'm pretty sure he isn't going to win any MENSA awards anytime soon.

We talked to the harbormaster who was nice enough to wave the docking fee and let us park along shore. He (thankfully) knew of the Trail and was willing to help out. He also told us of a film crew that had been here filming the arrival of one of the kayakers, the first we had heard that a celebrity was on the Trail. He said there was a big to-do about him, but he wasn't sure exactly why.

"Why aren't they filming us?" Andy asked, but he just laughed. I guessed we just weren't as important.

The Clyde began gently enough as we continued upstream (Turns out they dredged and straightened the lower part) but quickly steepened and grew rockier. We portaged perhaps a mile around several sets and a dam before crossing Clyde Pond and getting into the toughest upstream stretch of the trip. Three miles of continuous Class II rock gardens stretched before us. We simply dragged the canoe up foot by foot, stumbling over rocks and banging our shins and toes on every little outcropping. We slipped and slid, splashing into the water frequently and drenching ourselves. Several fishermen watched as we slowly clambered past, grinning sly grins as if to say, 'What in tarnation do these nimrods think they're doing?'

One voiced it with the oft-mentioned, "You know it's easier going the other way."   We still hadn't thought up a good reply so I just glared, and he quickly became deeply concerned with his fishing. It was also a foul-smelling river, and the smell of manure and pesticide dogged us for its entire length. And speaking of tires, there were dozens. By the time the Clyde was finished, the tire game score read something like 80-50, and I was frequently ignoring tires in an effort to let Andy catch up and make the game interesting again. There were spells where the word 'tire' resounded repeatedly for minutes at a time as we crossed tires that were all but stacked up along the river bed. The Clyde River is anything but a wilderness river, and we didn't drink out of it either.

We finally made it to the top, however, and after crossing Salem and Little Salem Lakes (and grounding once on a sandbar that did little to improve our grumpy mood, the result of being tired and dirty), we camped on the side of the river in a slightly swampy piece of land. Dry wood abounded, however, and our dispositions quickly turned sunny as we watched the saintly combo of dogs and beans cook. We went to bed bruised but full, confident that tomorrow would bring gentler currents.

June 21st, Day 17 – Clyde River to the Clyde River and Cold Brook: We awoke for our first full day on the Clyde and were paddling by eight in the morning. We portaged several dams quickly and found ourselves on the Upper Clyde, a completely different river from the lower part. It was gentle and twisted as we wound our way upstream, paddling several miles for every mile of progress made as the crow flies. It was quite boggy and marshy, and several herons greeted us as we rounded river bends. Otter played nearby, and hawks soared on the rising thermals above us. The land was covered in green bushes and grass, and beaver sign was everywhere, their peculiar hourglass brand left on many trees at their base when the beavers apparently gave up halfway through a tree and moved on to chew easier trunks. The river flowed slowly but cleanly, and the river bottom was as clear as day, the waves and ripples in the sand guiding us onwards. We frequently had to navigate around fallen trees and brush, going over submerged logs and under trunks bridging the river.

"It doesn't get much better than this, does it Sam?"

"Nope. It's so serene and cool, and peaceful too. You know what?"

"What?"

"This!" and I leaped out of the boat into the water. I needed to cool down.

We stopped briefly at a general store to refill our water bottles and buy some Cokes, and got lost briefly when I convinced Andy that the main channel we were following was actually not the river we were supposed to be on. I of course was wrong and we retraced the same part of the river several times before simply continuing on as we originally had done.

A group of canoes appeared ahead of us, and materialized into a nature group out for the day. None of them were adept at paddling and one duo looked particularly ineffective at steering their boat.

"Stay away from us!" one sternman giggled. "We can't steer so we might hit you."

"You guys aren't trying to go too far, I hope?" I asked.

"No. We're just out for the afternoon on a nature paddle, to see what we can see." The speaker was probably their leader since he seemed to be able to steer a little better. "How far are you going?"

"To Maine!" Andy shouted.

"Well alright, good luck. Be careful up ahead. The channel becomes harder to follow, and you'll probably get turned around at some point. But don't worry. With some searching you'll find it."

Thanking him, we left the group chuckling at their own inadequacy. We felt confident that we would be able to stay in the channel, and after another half hour of paddling we were just beginning to congratulate ourselves on our superior abilities when it became clear we were lost again. We circled several times going over the same piece of river, but were quite confused. At one spot, we were sure we were on the main river, still moving upstream, but as we continued to try and follow the main channel, it simply dwindled quickly into a feeder stream, Cold Brook, with no apparent turn offs in between.

It was towards the end of the day, and sure that we were not going to solve this dilemma while still in the boat, we found a flat spot of land along Cold Brook and set up camp. We then continued to follow Cold Brook upstream on foot to where it crossed Rte. 105, just to be absolutely sure we knew where we were, then walked along Rte. 105 and then Five Mile Square Road to where it crossed the Clyde further upstream, and there the Clyde was, just as it should be, flowing wide and clear. So somewhere in between here and our camp it must connect, but where?

We retraced our steps along Rte. 105, catching up with a would-be hitchhiker.

"How are you doing?" Andy asked. The man was red-faced and puffing from walking along the road, and clearly out of shape.

"My friggin' car broke down, and now no one will pick me up."

"Sorry to hear that. Vermont is a pretty friendly place though. Someone will get you."

"And it's so friggin' hot out. I wish it was god damn winter right now."

A truck came barreling down the road, but the man ignored it. He was too busy complaining to us, although, incredibly, he had not asked us what *we* were doing walking on a country road shirtless with life vests on.

To our surprise and the big guy's relief the truck pulled over on its own accord. The driver stuck his head out and offered us a lift. The man immediately began to jog (actually lumber) towards the car, his red face gleeful as he waved good-bye to us. It was certainly the first time I've ever seen an unsuccessful hitcher become successful without any outward sign he was interested in a hitch. We may have witnessed a mini-miracle. I wasn't sure.

We continued on and not five minutes later a van pulled over and asked us for directions to Five Mile Square Road. Amazingly, that was the one road in the entire state we knew of, since we had just been there five minutes ago, and we pointed him in the right direction. Remarkable.

We returned to camp, and I left Andy to make dinner while I set out to continue to look for the missing river. I set a course from our camp towards a nearby peak, Dolif Mountain, between which I knew the river must cross. Unfortunately, it was all swampland and I alternated between forcing my way through thick marsh grass and sinking knee-, thigh-, and even chest-deep into thick mud. Sure enough, however, the missing river appeared before me not ten minutes into my trek. I retraced its route downstream, finding that at the point where we lost it, it broke into several tiny channels, most of which were blocked securely with beaver dams and debris, and one of which was well-hidden. I marked several landmarks along the section of river we *could* find, and returned to camp confident that we could continue to follow the river's course tomorrow.

Dinner was just about ready and the chicken fajitas were fantastic. It took a little extra prep-work but the fresh lettuce and tomato were delicious and we enjoyed the meal, stuffing ourselves to the gills. Our frustration with being lost had given way to relief that we knew where to go again, and I fell asleep content with another obstacle overcome.

June 22nd, Day 18 – Clyde River to the Nulhegan River near Wenlock: The usual rigmarole of the morning got us on the river at the usual time. I had been arising earlier and earlier, regularly around 5 or 5:15, and was getting in lots of peaceful reading and relaxation in before waking Andy. Like I said, it was my favorite time of day.

We found the channel I discovered last evening with no trouble, aided by my landmarks, and continued on our way. The river narrowed and the channel became clogged with trees more frequently, causing me to bring out the axe occasionally to hack through limbs and trunks. I loved the power of an axe, the solid thwack as I brought it down with all my force on the tree, sending a shower of wood chips and fragments into the air. I got into a steady rhythm, causing the wood to fly, and they drifted alongside me on either side as the rhythm continued. Thwack! Thwack! Thwack! My cut became deeper, and eventually the tree split in two. I panted, standing in the water with sweat streaming down my back, and felt the thrall and happiness of the woods wash over me as the loose tree branch drifted downstream, a path now cleared for the canoe to continue.

We were sidetracked briefly right on the edge of Island Pond, the town, mistaking a swamp for the main current, but quickly re-found the channel and paddled *underneath* the Clyde River Hotel, getting a close look at the aging foundation.

Island Pond was a small but cheerful town and we enjoyed our quick visit, buying supplies and a new trowel since our old one broke. As we walked into the grocery store, my eyes set on a peach pie (my favorite) for the unbelievable price of $4.85. We sat out front for the feast, but after one bite I found it to be very disappointing and not the homemade pie I had taken it to be. I tossed most of it in the garbage, and made Andy promise to never let me buy a store-made pie again.

We crossed Island Pond, the pond, and unloaded for a 3.3 mile portage which was all the more unfortunate since we had just resupplied and had full wannigans, but it couldn't be helped. The first half was along a dirt ATV trail through a park, and the mosquitoes were quite bad for us. Surprisingly though, when I portaged with the canoe overturned on my shoulders they didn't seem to bother me, instead preferring to buzz around at the bottom of the boat (now the top since it is inverted), much as they buzz in the upper recesses of a tent when they sneak in. They never did manage to figure out to simply drop a foot and get me while I was helpless. It was only on the return walk, and later, with the wannigan and tarp, that they really bothered me.

The second half was along a road, and once again an older couple stopped and asked for directions. First the wife leaned across and asked, "How far have you carried that canoe?"

I answered, "A couple miles."

"How much farther are you going to carry it?"

"Another mile or so." I grinned. "You want to help?"

She just shook her head. Then they asked me what road we were on, and I answered. They were looking for a different one so I explained to them they had missed the crossroads back in the town of Island Pond (I had happened to note the two roads crossing there). Once again I passed for a local who knew the town like the back of my hand, but I think they drove off thinking me a little crazy for all the canoe portaging I was doing.

Several logging trucks also passed perilously close, sucking me into their vortex as they blew past, the canoe acting as a bit of a sail. I learned to give the trucks a wide berth, walking far out into the grass at the edge of the road to avoid being drawn into their wake.

But finally! Downstream again! We broke into spontaneous song and practically flew down the river. It was the headwaters of the Nulhegan and we were finally moving as everyone had told us to move: downstream.

Since it was the headwaters, the river was extremely narrow and also frequently doubled back on itself, its snakelike contortions of oxbows meaning that we were often slammed into the bank as the canoe failed to keep up with suddenness and violence of the river turns, despite our best efforts.

"O god! The branches again!" as we passed the shore too closely and alders raked across my body. I just laughed in the back.

"And spiders! I've got, what, four or five running around in the bottom here."

"You better hope they're not poisonous!" I could barely get out for the helpless giggles that racked my body.

"The branches – yuck. Patooie. Cobwebs in my mouth. And my eyes. I think I'm going blind."

"Charge!" I yelled and we raced ahead full steam, surmounting another beaver dam before getting tangled again in the bushes.

Amid cursing and laughing we continued on, enjoying the feel of the current working with us instead of against.

We passed East Mountain, atop of which is a radar base, a remnant from the Cold War. In 1961 an unidentified flying object was seen from the radar base, several hours prior to the time when Betty and Barney Hill claimed to have been abducted by aliens. Theirs was the first widely publicized alien abduction case and has gone on to become one of the most famous as well. Hypnotism sessions and extensive interviews went on to detail the abduction, and most evidence appears to prove that the Hills truly believed they were abducted. Whether aliens actually gave them a tour of their spacecraft and extracted samples of hair, skin, and blood is up for each individual to decide (Friedman and Marden 2007).

The shadows began to lengthen however, and a campsite was not to be found. Swamp and marshland surrounded us, and little hope appeared for a dry campsite. Then ahead in the distance, an island of pines appeared. We would draw close to it only to have the river abruptly bend away, then again switch back to near it, only to turn away again. We stopped on the side tantalizingly close, but when I tried to hike towards it, I found open puddles of water blocking the path. We continued onwards, nearly giving up hope, when Andy spotted a small side channel towards it.

"Let's try that," he said.

I shook my head doubtfully but steered us into to it, and voila! It led directly to the pines. We easily scrambled up a steep twelve-foot bluff to a flat area on top, which had clearly recently been logged. There were plenty of tent spots, and tons of down, dry wood, the remnants of a logging company, and we felt as though we had found a camping Eden in the swampy wilderness.

June 23rd, Day 19 – Nulhegan River to the Connecticut River near Masons: I listened to the beavers splashing and slapping their tails in the water as I made breakfast this morning. They certainly are active. We chased families of ducks down the river, their little feet paddling the water furiously in an attempt to get away from the big green monster bearing down on them. I didn't help things by growling at them.

"Arrrghhh. Here I come little ducky. Aren't you going to make a tasty morsel? Nom nom nom nom. You know what my favorite breakfast is? Raw duck l'orange. And it just so happens I have an orange here to go with you, so here I come." Of course I didn't have an orange, but how were they to know? It was just a good thing the ducks didn't understand English, otherwise they wouldn't have slept for a month.

The most amusing part was when the mother would give the signal to dive under. Then all the ducklings would throw their rear ends into the air, and they would hang there for half a second, like synchronized swimmers, before managing to submerge themselves. One little guy got separate from his family when they hid and he kept running, and we chased him for almost a mile before finally passing him. We kept trying to hug the shore farthest from him in an attempt to let him hide and return upstream to his family, but he was too skittish and it wasn't until a particularly wide section that we managed to pass him.

At first the river was as narrow and windy as yesterday, and the speeding current slammed us into alders and bushes again, covering us in spider webs, twigs, and spiders. The spiders promptly began to rebuild their webs in the boat, and when we stopped later on we had to do a miniature eradication campaign to clean up the boat. We scooped twigs out by the handful, and tossed the spiders overboard, returning the boat to its original capacity of only two travelers instead of the dozen or so stowaways we had managed to take on.

The Nulhegan, like many rivers, was used as a logging highway, and each spring huge log drives took place. On the Nulhegan, however, since it was a smaller and windier river than many used, it was especially important to time the different log drives to not interfere with each other and so prevent horrific logjams, so the loggers built semaphore towers on hilltops to signal to each other when to release which logs (Northern Forest Canoe Trail 2005).

The river began to widen as tributaries increased the flow, but it remained quite spiny, and we were forced to line several parts to avoid scarring the boat too badly. We portaged a mile around some larger rapids along a road, and on the first load passed a woman putting up a sign that said 'Sale Inside' in front of a store called 'Caron's Discount Store'. Thinking perhaps it had food, we stopped on our walk back and talked to a man who had just pulled up in front of the store.

"How are you doing?" Andy asked.

"Just fine. What are you guys up to?"

"We just portaged down the river here, and are heading back to grab our second load of gear. But we thought we'd stop in here first."

He laughed. "Don't bother. This store has been closed for years. The sign out front fool you? My mother, that's the lady who used to run the place, just keeps it up for nostalgia. Besides, all it sold was furniture and some old antiques. Nothing a couple of paddlers like yourselves would be interested in."

Thanking him, we continued on our way. We didn't ask about the 'Sale Inside' sign the woman had just put up. Perhaps she was going a little senile, or it was just ingrained habit. Who knows? It fooled us.

We stopped at the junction of the Nulhegan and the Connecticut, thankful to be done with the bumping and grinding, and walked down the road to the local general store (all that was there) to buy supplies and lunch. I finished a roast beef sub in seconds flat, and had to eat a peanut butter and jelly as well to fill up. It's hard work having so much fun on the river.

North Stratford, where we were now, saw perhaps one of the most unusual visitors to the North Country near the turn of the century. An Eskimo named Minik Wallace arrived on the train, the end of the line, headed for the lumber camps where he would work for the remainder of the year before succumbing to influenza. He was born in Greenland circa 1890 and was brought along with his father and four other Eskimos to New York City by explorer Robert Peary in 1897. His father and three others promptly died of tuberculosis since they had no natural resistance to the disease, but Minik managed to survive. He tried to bury his father but the American Museum of Natural History would not give up his body, refusing to even acknowledge that they had it. The Museum instead wanted to keep it for study and display. Peary had abandoned Minik in the city with no friends and little support, and also refused to support Minik's attempts to regain control of his father for proper Eskimo burial. The Museum eventually put on a fake burial, but Minik discovered the ruse several years later and resumed his efforts to see to his father, now on display in the museum as an Eskimo skeleton. Failing once again, he tried to see Peary about the promised return trip to Greenland. Peary continued to ignore Minik's well-being, although he eventually did return Minik, penniless, to his homeland twelve years after removing him. His people welcomed him although he had forgotten his own language and much of his culture and traditional skills. Minik however, did not feel at home, and in 1916 he returned back to the U.S. He felt welcome neither in Greenland nor the U.S. and had truly become a homeless wanderer (Harper 2000).

He worked at a number of jobs including several brief stints on stage acting as an Eskimo before being recruited through an employment agency for work in the lumber industry of northern New Hampshire. He took the train to the end of the line in North Stratford before taking a wagon to the lumber camp. Here he spent only one year before succumbing to the Spanish flu, but it proved to be the happiest of his life. He befriended a local farmer and found that at last he was at peace. He was treated as one of the family, and it was the only time of his life that he was not a spectacle to be gawked at. His body remains interred in Pittsburg, New Hampshire. He never recovered his father's body, and it was not until 1993 that it was returned to Greenland by the American Museum of Natural History (Harper 2000).

We continued downstream on the Connecticut, a wide and fast-flowing river which allowed us to move with little effort at high speeds (well, high speed for a canoe). It was great to be paddling on a river where, with little effort, you could make six or seven miles an hour. There were few rapids and those that did exist were easily navigated. It made for a quick and extremely enjoyable afternoon, and we arrived early at our campsite for the night next to an old railroad trestle. It was the first official campsite in a while, and the picnic table and outhouse were nice amenities. We even got a swim in, and scrubbed off several days of accumulated grime before turning in.

Chapter 6: Upstream Again - The Ammonoosuc, Androscoggin, and Rapid Rivers.

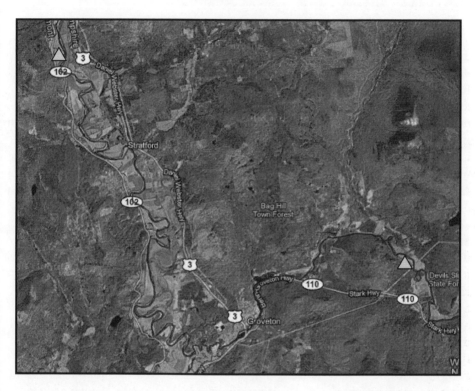

June 24th, Day 20 – Connecticut River to the Ammonoosuc River near Stark, New Hampshire: We awoke to a few slugs and a few bugs, but nothing too serious. As we paddled off we waved good-bye, thanking the youth crew who built it only several years ago.

In spite of the Connecticut being a popular river to travel on, and the plethora of houses and farms lining its banks, wildlife abounded and hawks soared above us as we made our way downriver. Colonies of bank swallows lived in the high banks, zipping in and out of the holes that they live in with surprising speed. The holes are only about two inches in diameter, so I am amazed that the birds manage to slow down once they get inside them, since they are cruising as they enter, but I assume they aren't slamming into the back wall every time they go home, so they must have some method. We also watched a deer drinking from the river. He didn't notice us until we got quite close, and he bounded away into the woods as soon as he scented us. Seconds later, a shot rang out! Andy and I looked at each other in surprise, then grinned.

"That deer sure bought the farm."

"Yeah. No kidding. Ouch."

"Andy, I'm not sure it's hunting season."

"No, I don't think so either. Tough luck for the deer then, right?"

Chuckling while looking over our shoulders to make sure the hunter didn't decide to chase the witnesses, we paddled on.

Logging occurred along these rivers as well. The Connecticut, with its feeder rivers of the Nulhegan and Upper Ammonoosuc, was often so filled with logs that sometimes the water beneath was not visible. Jams led to navigational problems, and bridges could be damaged from the pressure, such as the Nulhegan Bridge in 1894 which collapsed into the river along with a train when a jam undermined the bridge supports. The river drivers who rode the logs downstream were not the only ones with dangerous jobs.

We turned back upstream on the Upper Ammonoosuc around noon, and our speed was dramatically cut. We navigated rapids, doing some lining again as well as dealing with river wide strainers which needed to be negotiated with care. We ducked under one, but a stray branch caught my hat and flung it back downstream. I let out a shriek of despair, only half-acting, and jumped into the icy cold river. I didn't want to lose *another* hat. It took my breath away and I came back into the boat, with my hat, shivering. Thankfully, the sun quickly recovered my temperature equilibrium.

We portaged three dams, all short walks, and stopped in Groveton to read the NFCT kiosk and look at the old locomotive and caboose posed on the riverbank. It was used to ship lumber south in addition to the river drives. Finding little else of interest we continued on, disgusted by the sprawling complex on river right. It was the Wassau Paper Mill, the only one left around, and its grime streaked walls, cement stacks pointing skyward, and overall stench did nothing for our palates. However, there was little movement and it appeared to be silent. Since this was midafternoon on a Wednesday it gave us hope that the mill was failing and would perhaps be closed soon, if it wasn't already.

We continued upstream, cursing mightily as our shins and toes felt the brunt of the work. Several peaks off to our left rose spectacularly from the river basin, their steep cliff faces and rock slides providing a magnificent contrast to the greenery framing, and as the river flattened out and we were able to paddle more than line, our sunny dispositions and overall good humor returned. Nothing like the great wild woods, and the sight of river and mountains yet unclimbed (at least by me) to put me in a pleasant mood.

We camped at another campsite, the Frizzell campsite, and celebrated sit-down johns for two nights in a row with macaroni and cheese. I set the fire grate up poorly and the pot tipped over mid-boil, but we salvaged it, and we both agreed that the addition of a little pine-needle-after-taste to the meal was a culinary secret. Well, perhaps not, but it still went down smoothly anyways.

Examining the map after dinner, we came to an itinerary conflict. Andy was in favor pushing hard the next day by paddling twelve miles upstream and then attempting to do the four mile portage that afternoon. I wanted to attempt a more conservative approach since I was not interested in doing a long portage at the end of a day of hard upstream-paddling, and since we had no idea if the river would be gentle or require lining. I won out, due more to my stubbornness than any great debating skills, and we went to bed ready to take it easy the next day.

June 25th, Day 21 – Ammonoosuc River to the Ammonoosuc River near West Milan: We awoke to clouds, similar to the past few days, but the sun poked through early on, and it turned into a bright, hot day, necessitating several swim breaks along the way. We were in and out of the boat for the first couple miles before stopping in Stark, NH where we planned to resupply. Stark, while a picturesque town with several buildings all built in the same style and painted white, had little in the way of a grocery store. We wandered down Main Street (and I use that term loosely), but the community center, museum, and library were all closed. A statue of General John Stark stood in a small green, for whom the town is named, and he looked gallantly over the buildings. A small plaque at the base stated his name, birth and death, a quick eulogy to the effect that he was the hero of the Battle of Bennington, which he was. Several thousand troops under Lieutenant Colonel Friedrich Baum were advancing into Vermont, then known as the New Hampshire grants, and were met by a ragtag force under John Stark. Before the battle began he is said to have announced, "Tonight the American flag floats from yonder hill, or Molly Stark sleeps a widow…" which is also written on the plaque. I seem to recall several sea captains saying similar things when faced with horrendous storms, so while they were brave words, I don't know that they were all that original. The defeat suffered by the Hessians combined with defeats at Oriskany and Saratoga forced Gen. John Burgoyne to retreat back to Canada and helped to stall the British yet again from cutting the rebellious colonies in half, much as Arnold had done the previous year at Valcour Island (Rose 2007).

After the war General John Stark returned to New Hampshire, becoming a small time statesman, and generally (no pun intended) keeping a low profile. The picturesque town where we stood was named for him in 1832, but alas, has not grown enough to include a general (still no pun) store.

We stuck out our thumbs and quickly found a ride back to Groveton and the eyesore Wassau Paper Mill. And we thought we had left that place behind forever. Still no activity. We ate sausage, egg, and cheese sandwiches and resupplied at a small general store and sat outside with a number of older men who were clearly regulars, and spent most of their mornings perched outside. A general heckling of among them ensued:

"Hey Joe, you get a new haircut?"

"Why yes I did."

"They didn't need to cut too much did they, with that big solar reflector you got in the middle there? You operating on green power now, with that solar panel?"

"Heh, you should talk. If you walked into a barber shop, they'd all laugh at you and do it for free."

A third one joins in, "I find the ladies like a good bald spot. It shows wisdom and class."

"Ha. Ha. What'd you do, mistake Nair for your shampoo?!"

General laughter ensued as the store owner walked out.

"Hey Bill, you gotta stop working so hard, I think all that stress is getting to you. You've got no hair left!"

"Ha, I oughta kick you off my chairs. Anyways, I've got more hair than all of you guys combined, and this waste of life here too!" grabbing his own son as *he* walks outside.

The five of them break into laughter, genially rubbing the tops of their heads as a sixth one pulls up in a convertible.

"Hey, nice car there Walter! You just get it?"

Poor Walter unsuspectingly falls for it. "Yup, just signed the lease yesterday." He beams with pleasure.

"Uh, Walter, you compensating for something? It seems the nicer your car get, the less hair you have."

"Ya, Walter, you should probably put the roof back on, otherwise your gunna get a sunburn. Leads to all sorts of nasty lumps and spots you know! It's already beet red, and it's not even 10 o'clock yet!"

That breaks them up, and they all sit there guffawing as Walter shakes his head sadly.

They all happily agreed that haircuts certainly were cheaper now.

Andy and I kept a low profile as we ate our breakfasts, our full heads of hair in stark contrast to their own sparse coverage, but we had trouble keeping our smiles off our faces. They made quite a scene.

We bought our groceries and hitched back to Stark with a young, good-looking man with tattoos running up and down his arms and a fashionable goatee. He told us of his plans to move to Costa Rica to grow coffee. When we asked what he did now, he told us he was the pastor for Stark, which just about floored us. He was an extremely nice guy, just a bit of a study in contrasts.

The rest of the day was mostly paddling steadily but slowly upstream, with only a few short lining sections. We passed the site of a World War II prison camp which held German POWs who worked cutting wood in the forest. I had no idea that Germans were held in the United States, but several of these camps dotted the North Woods during WWII and many were spread across much of the United States. The Germans were often surprised upon arrival at the Statue of Liberty and booming war economy since they had been told back in Germany that the Luftwaffe had destroyed much of the country. They were soon rid of their misconceptions, however, and bustled to camps that needed work. The timber industry was especially desperate for labor during the war since loggers often moved in droves to better paying jobs in the cities, leaving the mills quiet (Koop 1988).

It was a tough life, and a number of Germans escaped, but the relationship between the Germans, guards, and townspeople was basically sound. Indeed, as more and more Germans escaped (something easy to do after a day's work in the woods) the townspeople became used to keeping an eye out for them. Once they realized that they posed no threat – the Germans had nowhere to go since an ocean separated them from home – it became a bit of a running joke. Later, townspeople and Germans bonded over art, music, and Hollywood. Foreigners such as French-Canadians and Norwegians working in New Hampshire found Germans who spoke their own tongue and quickly formed friendships with them. By the end of the war the town of Stark and the German POWs had become used to each other, and many had formed relationships (Koop 1988).

In 1986 a reunion was held bringing surviving POWS and their families back to the town to remember the long ago time. There is no sign of the camp from the river, but probably foundations remain in the trees.

We rounded a bend and came across a woman sitting in a beach chair half-submerged in the water, reading. That is a brilliant way to spend a hot afternoon, and she looked very comfortable there. Her dog had never seen a canoe before and barked for all he was worth at the two-headed talking green monster that appeared, proving he was not much smarter than the ducks.

"Don't worry, he won't bite. He's quite friendly. He just doesn't understand what's going on."

He kept barking, and we stopped the canoe next to the lady.

"Where you guys heading?" She repeated the old joke, "You know it's in the wrong direction."

"Yes, yes, we know. We're paddling to Fort Kent, Maine."

"Jesus Christ, all the way to Maine?"

"Yes ma'am, on the Northern Forest Canoe Trail."

"The what?" she asked incredulously.

"The Northern Forest Canoe Trail," Andy repeated happily. "You're sitting in it."

"Well I'll be. To think I've lived here for fifteen years and never knew about it. I don't think I've ever seen anyone else on it."

"Well, it's only been around for four years, officially. So that's part of it. But keep your eyes open, you might see some more!"

"Good luck you guys." We left her mumbling in amazement over the distance to Maine. We were just pleased to be able to do a little PR for the Trail.

It was a lazy afternoon, and we stopped often to swim, arriving at camp slightly earlier than normal, in spite of the short day. The hitchhiking necessary to resupply negated the previous night's debate since it would have been nigh on impossible to hitch and resupply, paddle, and portage the four-miler in a reasonable time, so the short day was the right choice.

We settled in for bed after dinner, and as I was slipping into dream world, I awoke suddenly in a panic with the sound of a train bearing down on me like a maelstrom. I was half out of my tent ready to run for it before I fully awoke and realized that trains could go nowhere except where their tracks led, and I was most certainly not on the tracks. It passed by, thundering off towards its destination, but it took several minutes before my heart settled back down to something like a normal beat. This campsite was altogether was too close to the tracks for my own personal well-being.

June 26th, Day 22 – Ammonoosuc River to the Androscoggin River near Goose Pond: Heat-lightning and a little rain occurred throughout the previous night, but I awoke well-rested, in spite of the train incident.

A short paddle got us to the portage and we took the first load over before it got too hot. An osprey was nested high atop a telephone pole at the put-in, and he screeched and flew in circles above us until we left the gear and returned back along the road. He must be protecting some young ones, or else he is extremely territorial. In any case, we clearly made him uncomfortable being nearby.

We stopped at a general store on the way back (should have planned to re-supply here instead of Stark) and bought cold sodas. We sat for a while and people-watched (a large variety of certified rednecks entered and exited) before taking over the second trip.

As we ate lunch thunder rumbled in the distance. It grew nearer as we finished, and we were forced to sit tight for forty five minutes while it passed overhead, rainless, before being able to continue on our way.

The Androscoggin was much larger than the Ammonoosuc and we lined several Class II sets, hugging the shore, before portaging a short distance around a dam and crossing the Pontook Reservoir. The current was much stronger below the dam, but in most places we could at least get a full blade in the water so we could begin to take full strokes again, something that was tough to do on the Ammonoosuc.

We camped on the northern end of the small reservoir, amidst a colony of mosquitoes, and we ate dinner quickly before ducking into our tents to read the evening away. I finished Don Quixote by Cervantes and began a narrative of Arctic exploration, and reading these two books: one an often nonsensical story of the journey and adventures of two men through Spain, and the other a non-fiction book recounting an Arctic expedition gone wrong only served to heighten my enthusiasm for being out in the woods on my own trip and adventure. The traveling life is the one for me, and to be always on the move, to never know what is around the next bend, thrills me to no end. The fact that 99% of the time the view is simply more river that looks almost exactly what I just paddled in no way diminishes my enthusiasm for the trip, and I will never understand the people who ask me, 'Don't you get bored out there?' There is no way I will ever get bored "out there". The wilderness is forever bringing new sights and sounds, and new challenges, and reading about others' trials and tribulations on their own journeys and adventures only creates a desire within me to never stop tripping, and to always search out what is around that next bend.

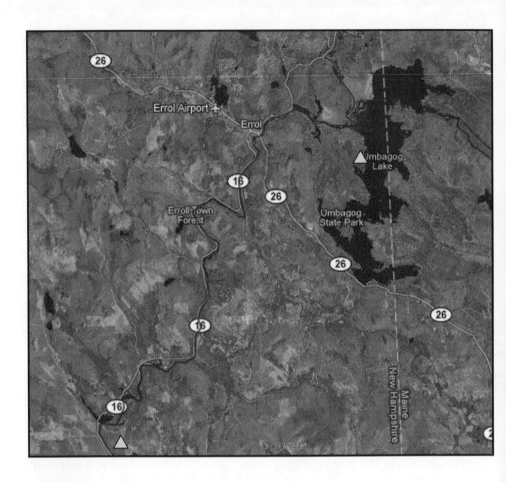

June 27th, Day 23 – Androscoggin River to Umbagog Lake: The sun was bright as we got an early start on the water. The section of the Androscoggin known as Thirteen Mile Woods stretched in front of us, with a dozen sets of whitewater marked, and perhaps more. We lined up two sets early on before being able to paddle several miles against a strong but not overwhelming current. Then it was into a long stretch of almost continuous whitewater. We moved slowly but surely, advancing steadily. Several sets right in the middle gave us significant amount of trouble. There, alders and bushes leaned far out over the river so we were forced to drag the canoe through them instead of around them since it was too deep where they ended. That took a lot of work, and we spent more time there than anywhere else.

At one point, as we paddled furiously, trying to advance from one eddy to the next, my top hand suddenly slipped off the top of my paddle, flinging the paddle grip straight back into my forehead and thwacking me hard. I let out a yell, leaned back for a second, then re-gripped the paddle and dug furiously into the water again, trying to gain momentum against the river. The wet grip and my wet hand did the same thing, and Thwack! I hit myself with my paddle again. Once again I yelled, and flew into a fury, the result of the pain in my forehead, and the embarrassment I felt at doing the same stupid thing twice. I smashed my paddle down on the gunwales as hard as I could. Unfortunately, my thumb was in between, and the shooting pains that shot up my arm quelled my rage almost immediately. Andy had by this time pulled the boat over to the side and was doubled over in laughter at my antics. I just licked my physical and emotional wounds and sulked for a minute, before taking a *much* better grip on my paddle and continuing onwards. Fortunately the incident failed to repeat itself for the rest of the trip. But it was not my best moment.

As we stopped for a snack and were munching on granola bars, we watched a pair of canoes attempt to run the rapids in front of us. They were both piloted by men with a woman in each of the bows, and they all looked woefully inexperienced. All four gripped their paddles by the shaft, not the handle, and they remained seated, dipping their paddles occasionally for some semblance of steering capability. We watched them enter the top of the set, betting on their immediate flip, but they hugged the bank and, since the set was only big water with no rocks, they avoided the waves and made it successfully to the bottom. We were amazed, but had to tip our hats to them. While they didn't do it in style, they didn't get wet either.

There were many others out on the water on this beautiful day, everything from large camp groups of five or six canoes to rowboats, to a sort of catamaran rowboat with one seat and two pontoons. The rower got quite wet sine there was no bottom to it, but there would have had to have been a hurricane to flip the thing. It looked relatively modern, and probably cost a pretty penny. Everyone, however, no matter what craft they were in, gave us funny looks, since we were the only ones heading against the current.

We stopped for lunch at a Subway in Errol, NH, sitting on the bench outside and watching caravans of motorcycles growl past. Some motorcades were made up of tough-looking characters who wore leather clothing, tattoos, bandannas over their hair, and sported large beards and mustaches while others were groups of retirees driving massive three-wheeled motorcycles with small trailers, complete helmets with walkie-talkie headsets and large, overstuffed seats and backrests. They wore complete color-coded rainsuits, and looked to be having the time of their lives. The remarkable differences between the two types were entertaining, and we spent almost an hour on the benches just observing the traffic through town.

The map showed a set of whitewater and dam adjacent to each other just north of town, but we found the dam to be further upstream so we portaged twice where the map shows just once, and paddled the last several miles onto Umbagog Lake. Just as we entered the lake, we watched a bald eagle perched atop a spruce tree. Suddenly a hawk wheeled from above and made several mock-dives at the eagle, screeching and dive-bombing it until the eagle flew to a different, nearby tree. This apparently wasn't far enough away for the hawk since he repeated the performance until the eagle flew off over the treetops, no doubt looking for more peaceful territories.

We camped at a campsite named Moll's Rock, a tribute to Molly Mollases who was the wife to the great chief Metallak. He was the last chief of the Coo-ash-aukes, the natives who lived in the area. They, weakened by disease and fighting, disappeared or were assimilated by other tribes and Metallak finished off his days poor and blind in Stewartstown, NH where he is said to have live to be 120 years old (Northern Forest Canoe Trail 2005).

It was a beautiful point, jutting out into the lake and providing 180 degree views of the surrounding waters and forests. We spent a pleasant evening reading and chatting, perched on the large rock and watching the sunset over the lake as a nice breeze tickled our necks.

"Andy, listen to the loons." They ululated in the distance, their eerie, ghostlike call spreading across the lake. Then thunder sounded.

"The thunder is responding. It's like the loons are calling for the thunder, and somebody up above is responding." And so it was. Every time a loon would call, the thunder would respond.

"I feel as though I'm eavesdropping on a cosmic conversation. Like this is something that has vast consequences for the future of the world, something that two small humans like us shouldn't hear."

The lonesome call of the loons continued, as did the low, distant, thundering response. We sat quietly, daunted by the magnitude of what was happening around us.

A small event of rather large repercussions took place as well. The day before, on the four-mile portage, Andy saw a wrench on the side of the road, but didn't think much of it. One sees trash, shoes, chairs, all manner of discarded objects – a wrench is no different. But half-a-mile further on, he saw another, of the exact same size. Thinking it fate, he picked it up and put it in his pocket. Today, one of the seat bolts was loose. I tried to tighten the nut with just my fingers, but had no luck. It was rusted onto the bolt and wouldn't budge. Andy walked up, and saw me struggling, 'Need a wrench?' He pulled it out of his pocket and handed it to me. It was a perfect fit. Perhaps there is a God.

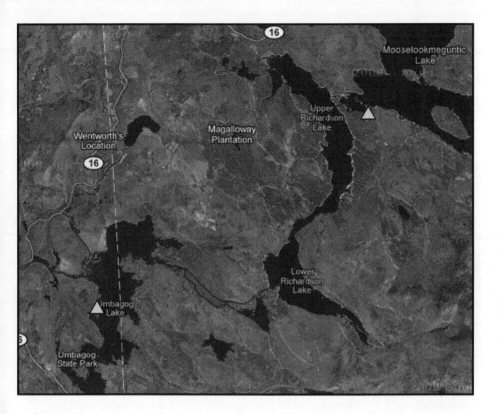

June 28th, Day 24 – Umbagog Lake to Mooselookmeguntic Lake, Maine:
Breakfast on Moll's Rock was just as nice as the evening before, and it boded
well for the rest of the day to have such a pretty start. The partly cloudy
conditions quickly deteriorated, however, and we were subjected to first mist,
then drizzle, then a full-on rain storm by the time we finally made camp.

We started out by quickly crossing Umbagog Lake before portaging 3 ½
miles up Rapid River. The Rapid is a fast, violent river with rapids ranging from
Class III to IV. We were happy to portage since it would have torn our canoe to
pieces, going up or down it. The portage followed a dirt road, little more than a
wide ATV track that cars could just barely make it down, and passed through a
tiny little hamlet made up of rough summer cottages and huts, and a tiny fly-
fishing shop. The shop was right next to the former home of best-selling author
Louise Dickenson Rich who wrote <u>We Took to the Woods</u>, a fascinating account
of her time growing up in the Maine backcountry. Asked what she wanted to do
when she grew up, she replied that she "was going to live alone in a cabin in the
Maine woods and write" (Rich 1942). It turns out she did just that, and the result
was a wonderful little book about growing up on the Rapid River. She described
eating "smitches and dabs" which is "a smitch of this and a dab of that,"

something that Andy and I can relate to (Rich 1942). We ate whatever happened to look good at the moment, often in slightly odd combinations.

Only slightly prior to Rich's time was another famous lady of the Maine woods, Cornelia Thurza Crosby. Better known as 'Fly Rod' Crosby, she was an expert fisherwoman and writer who spent much of her life advertising the Maine backwoods, and promoting tourism, hunting, and fishing. She toured the country showing everything from live animals to guides and native representatives at sportsmen's exhibitions across the country, befriending the famous Annie Oakley (Northern Forest Canoe Trail 2005).

Nodding our tribute to these ladies as we portaged past, we put in on Lower Richardson just past Middle Dam, where half a dozen fishermen were out pitting their skills against the local brook trout. We flew down the length of the lake and a quick portage later found us on Mooselookmeguntic Lake (say *that* three times fast). The portage was quite short but on it we passed the home of a third famous lady of the Maine wilderness, Carrie Stevens. She is known fishing-world-wide as the inventor of the Gray Ghost Streamer, a fly that she herself tied without ever having tied one before. She went fishing with it and promptly landed a 6 lb. 13 oz. brook trout, the biggest ever landed there to date. She went on to invent 24 other types of flies and to tie thousands more. She was rather secretive about the process though, and no one ever saw her finish one.

We paddled a mile across a small bay on Mooselookmeguntic against terrific headwinds and steady rain to camp for the night. We took our time unloading the boat, forced to be careful because of the waves breaking against shore and a tricky unloading zone, but once in the woods and among the trees, the air promptly became still. It was rather eerie watching the lake whipped into froth out in the center while all was still in the forest. We quickly set up camp and I got a fire going to begin dinner. Lighting a fire in the rain could be challenging, but I rather enjoyed it (especially when I succeeded). We enjoyed grilled cheese sandwiches doused in ketchup.

We sat under the tarp digesting dinner for a time, then Andy decided to rise for some reason, and he promptly proved that I, in spite of my clumsiness with the paddle the day before, was not the only klutz of the group. He simply tried to go from sitting to standing but got his legs tangled and promptly fell on his face. It was my turn to laugh. He did too, and we both got a good chuckle over our own idiocies. Keeping in good humor about everything and never letting ourselves get down was the key to a successful trip

Chapter 7: Into Maine – Across the Lakes and Down the Dead River

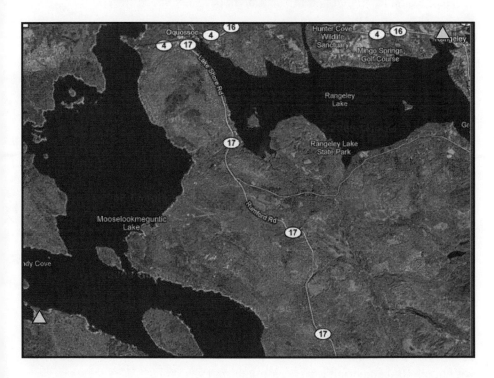

June 29th, Day 25 – Mooselookmeguntic Lake to Rangeley: We rose early in order to arrive in Rangeley in time for some lunch. It was still raining so we had to take down our tent, tarp, and pack and load up in it, but we dried it all out later in Rangeley.

Thick fog obscured all but a ten-foot radius around us as we began, but it gradually cleared as the day wore on. We rounded an island early on and saw nine canoes streaming across the lake, spread out over a half mile in a line. We stopped and talked to the first couple boats and found they were a school trip out from the University of New England. They were quite a sight as they swerved back and forth across the lake, paddling on the same side and tangling with each others' paddles. Later as we hugged the shore we chatted briefly with a family who was fed up with the rain and just wanted to go home. They need a little attitude adjustment. Rain should never upset anyone. There is no such thing as bad weather, just bad preparation.

The boat launch that marked the beginning of the portage into Rangeley Lake was a little difficult to spot among all the other houses and docks lining the shore, but we found it and began the first load along a road. Perhaps halfway through carrying the canoe, as I walked along the edge of the road, a car pulls up and the back window rolls down. Andy pokes his head out.

"Yo dude. I've got all the gear here. I'll meet you at the end."

The driver laughed and said to me, "Guess you'll have to walk. I can't take the *canoe* in the car!"

Andy gave me a slightly embarrassed shrug and they drove off. I fumed the rest of the way, furious that Andy would accept a ride. We had agreed at the beginning of the trip that all portages would be done under our own power. I walked quickly so I could reach the end and talk to Andy. I was really upset, and was planning to say all sorts of things to him when I got there.

I found him sitting on the wannigan.

"What the hell Andy? Why the hell would you take a ride? I thought we said we were going to do all this on our own? If you can't handle it, at least let me portage my own gear. You take the ride, but not me."

Andy held up his arms in defense. "Sam, I didn't have a choice. He just put it all in his car by himself, then drove up to me as I was walking on the portage, and told me to hop in. What was I going to do? I couldn't just leave the gear in his car, could I?!"

"You could have told him to drive it all back, and put it back where he found it! What the hell kind of person does that anyways – takes someone's stuff without asking?! Jesus Christ."

"I think he was just trying to be helpful…"

"Helpful – hell. He was a pain in the ass. We are doing a trail here. He should have asked. And you shouldn't have gotten in with him. Next time make him turn around and bring it all back to the start!"

But I was being wildly unreasonable to Andy which I realized as I was saying it, and soon afterwards I cooled down a little. It amazes me that someone would do this. I knew he thought he was being helpful, but ask first! I was, and still am, a strong believer in being true to a trail, which means doing every inch of it under one's own power, and this guy's attempt at help really frustrated me. Fortunately, this was the only incident we had like this, and though many people offer to help portage our gear with their car, we always refused.

The weather had cleared by the time we loaded again and got the canoe on the water, but the wind had increased, and we shoved off into extremely strong headwinds on Rangeley Lake. We dodged from cove to cove, hugging the shore and finding whatever shelter we could behind docks, rafts, moored boats, anything as we fought into the wind. We still took on water over the bow frequently, especially when we had to cross open bays, even though they were small, and the seven miles from the portage to Rangeley took almost three hours, and required three separate stops to bail the boat out. The canoe rode the waves well rocking steeply up and down and we shouted for joy as spray whipped in our faces and waves crashed into our laps. We finally rounded the point into City

Cove however, and the winds quickly died as we paddled across the small inlet to the town of Rangeley.

This was our first night in town where we actually would stay in town. We stopped at the Chamber of Commerce where they told us the cheapest motel in town cost more than $100, but we walked down the road to a low-cost-looking one, and found the price tag was only $70 for the two of us. Never trust the Chamber of Commerce I guess.

We checked in, spread our gear all over the room to dry, and pulled the canoe up and left it overturned behind the motel. Then we walked down Main Street, absorbing the sights and smells of town life. The first order of business was lunch, and we ate a massive meal of eggs, pancakes, home fries, and sausage at the town diner. Then we wandered back up the street, stopping briefly in one store to buy Andy a pair of camp sandals. Then to the local used book store where we perused for almost an hour, buying several. The remainder of the afternoon was spent relaxing, watching the boob tube, and listening to classic rock on the radio. It was good to hear my old friends Led Zeppelin, Van Halen, Styx, and the Rolling Stones again. One thing I do end up missing in the woods is good music.

Dinner was a large pizza for each of us, and ice cream for dessert while we waited for our laundry to dry. As we sat licking our cones, a float plane skimmed in over town, barely missing the tree tops and church steeples, and landed right in the city bay.

We fell asleep watching the baseball game, and I drifted off content when the Red Sox (I'm from Boston) beat the Orioles (Andy is from Baltimore). A good ending to a good day.

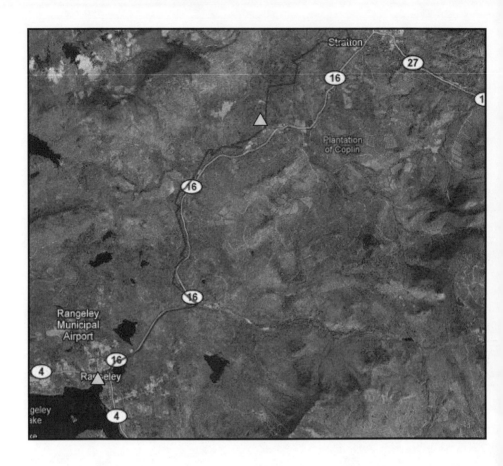

June 30th, Day 26 – Rangeley to Dead River near Langtown Mill: Although today was the day that we could sleep in and take our time in the morning, I awoke at my usual early time - my body too used to the morning routine. I read for a while on the back porch, looking out over misty Rangeley Lake, before taking another shower (since they come few and far between, you must always take advantage of the opportunity), and heading out to breakfast with Andy. I ate just as much, if not more, than yesterday, and felt quite bloated as we waddled back to the motel. A quick pack-up and we were on the portage trail again, four miles along the road. It was a painful four miles. My whole digestive system was operating on overtime, trying to process the immense amount of pancakes, eggs, bacon, and potatoes I had crammed down my throat, and it was not happy. Painful stomach cramps dogged me for the whole time, and it was with great relief that I finally set down the canoe on the far side, along the Dead River. I was able to rest for half an hour before Andy arrived, and that down time was essential to my recovery. By the time we walked back and began our second load I was much better, but I made Andy promise to never let me do that again.

The Dead River was far from dead. It was flowing several feet above its normal levels, and so we motored right along, again caroming off of trees and branches as we made our way downstream. We even managed a few shortcuts over normally solid ground as the river flowed over narrow oxbows, straightening itself out with its increased volume. Many trees were down, and brush occasionally clogged the way, but we were forced to use the axe only once to paddle onwards.

As we continued downstream the river sped up, and we ran some great rapids, going over waves and dipping deep into troughs, riding the river down. We took on water several times, once nearly swamping, but did not flip, and generally had a grand old time on the river. Andy in the front got drenched several times as the bow dipped under water, the cold water splashing over his front. I in the stern remained drier, but by no means was I dry.

A deer swam across right in front of us in one of the calmer sections, but struggled to get out of the water since the bank had become sodden underbrush. Later, the stink of decaying flesh came to our nostrils, and snarled in a strainer, a dead deer with overgrown toenails was stuck. He had clearly been there for several days, and probably got stuck trying to cross the river in even higher waters. Lucky for the second deer, he made it with only minimal trouble.

We camped on an island that appeared to normally be a peninsula, but with all the high water overflowing banks it became a large island. It was slightly marshy, but had good wood for a fire, and we found some good dry tent sites. It felt great to be out camping in the woods again.

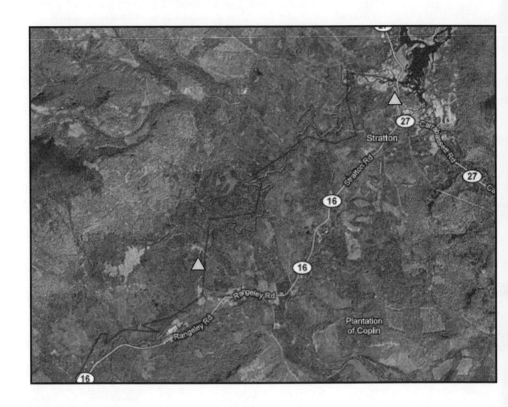

July 1ˢᵗ, Day 27- Dead River to Stratton: O Mamma Mia! What a day this one turned out to be! It started inauspiciously enough, with the normal routine, but barely fifteen minutes after getting on the fast moving river we clipped a submerged birch tree and flipped. No complicated maneuvers, no tricky whitewater to navigate, just a simple lapse of attention. I was in the bow, so I probably should have been the one to see it first, but in my defense it was submerged in the murky water and we didn't see it until the last second. It hit us amidships as we swung around in a turn around a river bend, and since we weren't on our knees like we would be in whitewater, our center of balance was high and over we went.

      The water was freezing, and left us gasping for breath as we pulled the gear to the side. Like the deer the day before, we struggled to find a spot on the bank where we could get out, but eventually Andy scrambled up a steep, brush-free area, and while I stayed in the water gasping with the cold, we managed to get most of the gear out of the water. We flipped the canoe back upright, struggling to do so since even along the bank the water was too deep to stand, reloaded, and continued downstream, wet and slightly bitter, but none the worse for the wear. I had let go of my paddle in the effort to save the gear, but we picked it up further along as it floated. The marshy lowlands that the river had been flowing through gave way to rockier, steeper banks which quickened and whitened the water. Small ledges began to appear as the waves grew bigger. Rocks and strainers began to appear, making the run more technical. We navigated successfully for a time, scouting once, and continued on. But the banks continued to grow rockier, we took on more water, no eddies appeared to pull off into, and suddenly, as we moved right to left and tried to swing around a rock, we clipped it, and flipped again. This time was worse, much worse. The rapids had been continuous for the last several miles, and they gave no sign of letting up. With no way to swim the canoe to the side, we simply rode it out. Andy was in front of me, and I could see his head bob in and out of the waves as he sputtered for air while being ducked under repeatedly by the waves. I was fortunately already upstream of the canoe, so simply turned on my back with my feet downstream, and watched Andy and the sunken canoe buck and bash on rocks and the bottom as it tumbled through the whitewater. It would be floating along, submerged, and would suddenly shoot into the air as some hidden rock forced it upwards. I winced often, not only for the beating the canoe was taking, but also for the one I was as well. All those rocks the canoe hit I did as well, and I came out of it with massive bruises along my butt and thighs.

Perhaps a 1/3 of a mile further downstream the river finally slowed enough to allow us to swim up to the canoe and drag it into an eddy. We turned it over, and were horrified. A massive dent bent in the floor of the canoe, but with a few kicks it bent back out to where it should be. More worrisome was the gunwales. Rocks had hit the left gunwale between the stern and center thwart, and between the center and bow thwart, and instead of curving nicely out, there were now two sharp dents inwards, the gunwale broken in several places, and it was generally chewed up along its entire length. Very worried now, but with little ability to repair the gunwale here, we climbed back in and paddled out into the river to try and recover some stuff.

The next half hour was spent paddling back and forth across the river, avoiding some rocks and hitting others, as we tried to collect all our stuff. Both wannigans had opened up as we floated down, and stuff was everywhere, floating down the river. We silently gathered two wannigans, one lid, numerous food bags, my water pump, the stove fuel bottle but not the stove, and various other things including one cup, some more food, and the duct tape. But the list of unfound things was staggering. We were missing the one wannigan lid, which had my tent, the tarp, the axe, and my water bottles attached to it. We were missing Andy's tent as well, and his first aid kit. Both wannigan tump lines were gone, as well as anything heavy that had been in the gear wannigan including our pot and pan, my stove, the grate, and other, smaller things. What a flip this one turned out to be. How innocently we had been paddling, with few proper measures taken to protect against this. We should have secured the wannigan lids better, we should have tied down the gear to the boat, we should have… Lots of 'should-haves'.

Once we had collected everything in sight, still paddling through numerous Class IIs, we stopped in an eddy to see if anything else would drift down. The cup, pump, and duct tape all did drift directly into our eddy (it was a big one) and we fished them out of the water. After waiting a while and seeing nothing else, we continued to the bottom of the rapids, all the rapids, and pulled over to the side to regroup. Our food consisted of peanuts, bread, pepperoni, and not much else so we sat on the side of the river on this calmer section, eating pepperoni sandwiches and peanuts, and waiting to see if anything else would drift down the river. We waited half an hour, saying little, but found nothing. My anger and frustration, directed at Andy, the river, the situation, myself, everything, began to cool. I had banged my left thigh quite hard and the muscle had tensed up so I was limping fairly severely as I walked. It would remain like that into the next day.

We were frustrated, depressed, upset, and trying to think about how to go on. The town of Stratton was only a few miles away at the outlet of the river onto Flagstaff Lake, so we decided to go there, spend the night in town, and try to find somewhere to buy new tents, pots, etc. It was the best we could do, and there was no way I or Andy was going to quit, no matter how much it cost. But we would be more careful in the future, more judicial in our selection of which rapids to run and which to portage, more conservative in our choices, and more careful of our gear and our bodies.

Nothing else floated past our perch on the grassy bank, so we reluctantly climbed back into our canoe, faced with the prospect of a very expensive resupply, and paddled the last few miles onto the lake and into town. The boat launch was simply a dirt road into the water, and we stashed our canoe in some nearby woods, along with the wannigans and little gear we had left. Our personal dry bags, fortunately still with us, we carried into town.

Stratton was a small town with a Main Street of only a few shops. We stopped first at the Stratton Motel and dropped our gear off in the attached hostel. The owner, Sue, was very friendly and sympathetic to our plight, and set us up with no problem. The hostel was very nice and cozy with a number of beds, family room, kitchen, and shower. One could ask for nothing more.

We walked over to a sort of hunting outdoors store to see what they might have for us. It turned out little, but they said there would be a massive Fourth of July sale in Rangeley the next day at a number of outdoors shops. We decided to go there, and returned to the hostel to loaf and recuperate for the remainder of the day.

We watched "Pulp Fiction", read, and generally did very little for the remainder of the day (we had arrived in town around noon), allowing our egos and tempers to get back to their normal ranges. It had been an extremely tough morning, and it took a while for my heart to slow down and heightened senses to return to normal levels.

As I sat on a bench right outside the motel, a massive, oversized load came through town, led and trailed be several vehicles escorting it. It carried a section of the tower for a wind turbine, and was headed for nearby Kibby Mountain where a wind farm was under construction. The truck that carried it was almost twice as long as a normal semi, and the tower section took up most of it. And that was only a section! I had been to a wind farm before, so I knew they were massive structures, but seeing one on a truck going through a small town was amazing. I am a huge proponent of wind power, worked on several projects for a non-profit promoting wind power at one point, and watching the tower section, and later a blade and a generator, go by, improved my mood immensely.

Several Appalachian Trail thru-hikers also spent the night, and catching up with them was fantastic. I thru-hiked the AT in 2008 so we compared notes on the Trail and talked about all our favorite spots to stop along the way. That trip down memory lane was another boost to my mood, and by the time Andy and I went to bed, after several pounds of steak (they were selling some pretty good cuts for 1.99/lb at the general store) for dinner, my mood was restored. Andy too was feeling much better by evening. He generally bounced back more quickly from downturns than I did. The fact that we had a plan with promise did wonders to our moods, and if we had gone to bed with nothing to look forward to on the following morning, I think we would have had a much different atmosphere. As it was, it had been an extremely trying day, but we hadn't given up, and we were prepared to face the next one head on, with smiles on our faces. You've got to always look forward, no matter what comes your way.

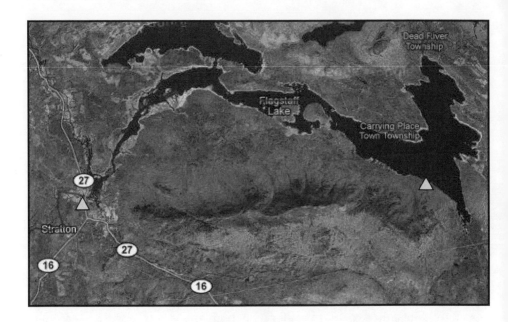

July 2nd, Day 28 – Stratton to Flagstaff Lake: We slept in a little (the sale didn't begin until 10) and then ate at the diner across the street. While munching on eggs and pancakes, we perused the local paper and were happily surprised to stumble on an article about the Northern Forest Canoe Trail! There was a picture on the front page of one of the kayakers out in front of us, and the paper described briefly the Trail and its history, and then went on to detail a description of Gil, attempting the first thru-paddle by kayak, and also attempting to become the oldest man to do it. It was fantastic to see the Trail get some press, and we were cheered with the thought that we were among the pioneers of this trail, with few others to have attempted or completed it before us. Our only regret was that they didn't write an article on us. After all, we were extremely interesting guys, not to mention our roguish good looks.

We caught the first car that passed back into Rangeley (quickest hitch I've ever gotten) and rode for sixteen miles in the back of a pick-up. I love riding in the bed, with the wind streaming through your hair. Myself and one of the AT hikers were in the back, and Andy was up in the cab. When we arrived and waved good-bye to the driver, Andy told us that the driver was warning Andy that the end of the world was upon us, and that because of the destroyed ozone layer, greenhouse gas emissions, and other environmental problems that the human race did not have much longer. There were some crazy folks up in Maine, but at least he gave us a ride.

Once in Rangeley (we were *not* happy to see this town again), we did some shopping. We stopped at the grocery store for some plastic bowls and spoons, then onto a hardware store for a tarp, tumpline, rope, etc. We stopped at the 'big' outdoor sale only to find it rather small with mostly odds and ends of gear. There was only one tent, a one-man, so that wouldn't do for us. We stopped by an outdoors store, and found a two-man for $75, which was a pretty good deal, and it was a nice tent, so we bought it. After resupplying with the bare essentials, we hitched back to Stratton with a man who had worked on some of the upcoming portage trails. We were happy for his work, and he was excited that people were actually using the trails, so it was a good ride.

Back in Stratton we bought food supplies at the grocery store, pulled the canoe out of the underbrush, and got back on the water. On the Trail again at last! We backtracked westward almost a mile to the mouth of the Dead River where it enters Flagstaff Lake.

"I just want to take a peek, Andy. See if anything floated down overnight. You never know."

"I don't know Sam. Aren't we looking for a needle in a haystack? This is a pretty big river mouth, with lots of nooks and crannies. I don't think we're going to find anything."

"Humor me, big guy. Keep your eyes peeled. Remember, I'm colorblind so it's not going to stand out for me like it will for you."

We paddled slowly among some low island, our eyes straining for anything resembling our gear.

Suddenly, Andy pointed. "Over there, do you see that orange thing!?"

"Nope, but let's go see…"

We paddled over to the bank, and voila! A bag of granola bars floated among the weeds! And right next to it was Andy's tent! Hooray! We laughed and shouted, this small find making us gleeful within seconds. My hopes soared that we might find my stuff as well, but after a long period of searching, we found nothing. The fact that two separate things ended up in the exact same spot along the bank pointed towards the fact that we would find little anywhere else. Clearly the current was depositing things there that night.

But Andy had his tent back, and we paddled off in high spirits. We retraced our steps again, and finally, around noon, began to make forward progress on the day. We had been knocked down, but we got back up again, and kept going. We were still game, and something like a little flip was not going to beat us down for long.

The rest of the afternoon was spent on Flagstaff, paddling against fierce headwinds as we took water over the bow again. It wasn't as bad as on Rangeley Lake, but it still slowed us considerably.

I tried a small shortcut through a narrow passage between several islands that appeared to be open on the map. It turns out it was mired with tons of driftwood, stumps, and a black sludge. Instead of going back all the way around the islands, we opted to portage over the driftwood-sludge-mess. Hilarity ensued. We tried to hop from one log to another, avoiding the sludge, but would sometimes slip, sinking calf, knee, hip, or even chest-deep into the mud. At one point I was sitting in the canoe, with Andy next to me up to his chest in mud, begging for help. I was laughing so hard at his predicament that I was incapacitated, and Andy just stayed there, sunk, getting madder and madder, only several feet away but utterly stuck. I calmed down, took a picture of him in his helpless state, and then was able to help him out, but for the rest of the day the boat and Andy had a black sheen over them.

We got to camp on the side of the lake around five, and set up our new tarp with new rope and my new tent. We also made a new tumpline, and a lid for our new cooking pot out of a can of baked beans by cutting it open and flattening it. It would also serve as a frying pan. After lots of work manufacturing and setting up the new gear, it was just like old times. Back on the Trail, yee-ha!

Benedict Arnold also had to paddle here as part of his ambitious drive to attack Quebec City in 1775. However, it was still a river since the Long Falls Dam wasn't built until 1950. Arnold brought 1100 men up the Kennebec and Dead Rivers, across the Bigelows, and down the Chaudiere River to attack. Unfortunately, by the time he got there, his men numbered only 600 (most were sent back although some died of starvation and/or disease). They were worn out and starving as well as badly lacking in clothing and equipment. Like us, they had a lot of trouble with the Dead River. They were using bateaux which are much larger, unwieldy boats not suitable for the clogged waterways of Maine. They were leaky, heavy, and poorly constructed and they suffered much more than we did. The Patriots were severely delayed by the numerous setbacks encountered during the march and the blizzard that occurred as they made their attack only added to their troubles. The attack failed but it still remains one of the more ambitious campaigns ever undertaken to this day, especially in light of the poor technology, maps, and planning that went into the march. The fact that they even made it to Quebec will cause it to be forever remembered in the history books (Randall 1990).

Our typical out-of-town dinner of tube steaks (hot dogs) and baked beans went down smoothly, and then some windy star-gazing finished the night. We talked a lot about our M. O. for the rest of the trip, deciding to take fewer chances, portage more, scout more, and generally be more cautious and conservative in our approach to rapids. Neither of us could afford to replace all this gear again, and so we promised each other to rein it in, and keep a close eye on the risks we took. Above all, we wanted to finish the Trail in one piece.

Since Andy had his tent back, I slept alone in the new two-man tent, and was able to really spread out in the roominess. I slept well as the wind whipped branches back and forth overhead.

July 3rd, Day 29 – Flagstaff Lake to Spencer Lake: The wind was still blowing, though not as hard, when I woke up, and I had to build the morning fire partly into the woods to keep it sheltered. Flagstaff Lake was still throwing headwinds at us as we paddled across its width, but it calmed down once we were back on the Dead River.

The first portage was around Long Falls Dam, built in 1950 to regulate the flow of the Dead River (the previous days' water levels were proof that it could fluctuate significantly). Three small towns, Flagstaff, Dead River, and Bigelow, were required to be evacuated since they would be flooded by the new dam. A book entitled <u>There Was A Land</u> was published chronicling townspeople's memories of the towns. One remembered that the electric current produced only DC voltage, so all visitors were forced to use adapters. Another remembered riding to school in a big black skimobile in the winter instead of a bus when the snow got too high. A third recalled peddlers coming each year to sell goods to the remote villages, including "branches" of bananas, watermelons, and paintings of scenery – as if they didn't have enough scenery all around (Goodson 1999)! Supposedly roads from the now-underwater towns can still be seen at low water, something not viable after the rainy summer we'd been having, so we paddled on (Northern Forest Canoe Trail 2005).

We also portaged around Grand Falls which was especially impressive. We took several pictures of a fisherman casting his line into the mist at its base. He took no notice of us, and indeed could not have heard us if he had wanted to due to the roar of the falls. He simply stood there on a small rock near the shore surrounded by water, looking for all the world as though he had no worries. Someday I too, perhaps, can fish all day without catching a thing and go home a contented man.

We turned left onto Spencer Stream to go upstream once more, right at the access point where many rafting companies put their boats in. If we were to have continued further down the Dead River, Class IV and V rapids would have met us.

Spencer Stream was a shallow, fast moving stream perhaps 50 yards wide, and we did a lot of dragging up it. As we moved further upstream and moved onto a tributary, however, the water slowed and we were able to make better time. We surprised ourselves by being able to make it all the way to Spencer Lake. Our maps showed an old, washed out dam just as we entered Spencer Lake, but the dam looked to be working just fine when we rounded the bend. It was ten feet high and surrounded on both sides by steep rock. The portage was only 100 feet, but it was a crazy one as we struggled to keep our footing on the sharp, slippery rocks. We made it into Spencer Lake without accident, however, and paddled to shore nearby as rain threatened. Dark storm clouds rumbled as we set up camp and quickly gathered wood, built a fire, and began to cook, trying to beat the rain. We ended up camping on a small beach with several small tent sites carved out among the trees. An old fire ring was further proof it had been used some years before, but it clearly was not a common stop-over.

The macaroni was boiling and about halfway done when a sheet of rain came whipping over the lake. We watched in stunned silence as the strongest downpour of rain we had ever witnessed immediately doused our roaring fire, soaked everything in sight, and forced us to crowd under the tarp (Thank God we had bought a new one). The wind violently vibrated the tarp, but the grommets and rope held and so the tarp remained intact. I raced out into the rain, retrieved the half cooked mac & cheese, and we ate semi-hard pasta for dinner. Not particularly delicious but at least we ate.

With few options for enjoyment as the storm raged around us with few signs of letting up, we went to bed early. We simply put the cooking pot outside and it filled almost instantly with water, so the dishes were done. Our water bottles were easily filled in the same way from the water streaming off the tarp. It was really something to witness, and hear, since the thunder and lightening appeared to be almost overhead, and the sound of the wind bending and thrashing the trees with water was quite loud. Sleep was easy to attain, however, after the long day of hauling upstream.

Chapter 8: Across the Height of Land and Onto the Moose River

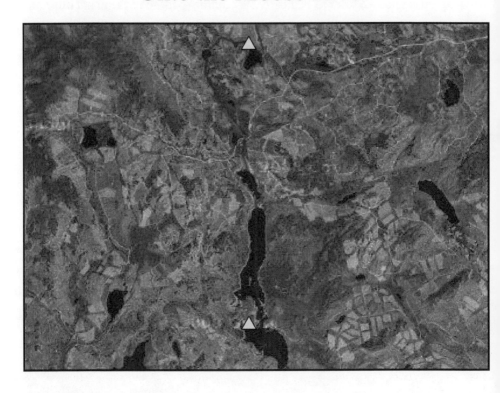

July 4th, Day 30 – Spencer Lake to Whipple Pond: We got up early, planning on trying to get near to the town of Jackman in the hopes that some fireworks would be in sight. Unfortunately, our plans failed miserably.

The day started off well enough. We paddled across Spencer Lake under cloudy skies. No rain fell, it all having poured out last night, so only a light breeze blew. We had to pull over once to repair the seat again. Since the 'tire game' appeared to be over, we began the 'fatty game', keeping track of who was sitting on the bow seat when the screws or string broke to see who was the biggest bucket of lard. I was winning.

It took us several minutes to find the outlet of the stream we were supposed to follow up, but we finally did, hidden among the reeds and water lilies. It began easily enough, and we wound our way slowly but steadily up the creek. It was barely ten feet wide, but quite deep right up to the banks, so there was no question of us getting out and dragging if we needed to. It would have been over our heads.

As we continued along, alders growing on the banks began to crowd closer and closer. Some began to hang across the entire stream, from both banks, forming an interweaving network of branches. We would paddle furiously, trying to force the canoe over or under branches, and drip sweat with the effort of only moving several feet, or even inches. We moved slowly, and the branches crowded tighter and tighter. Andy, in the bow, would get on his knees, lean out over the front, lift a partially submerged branch over the bow of the boat, then over himself. It would then be my turn to lift, forcing the branch up and over until it was finally past the boat. These branches were frequently quite heavy to lift as we forced them in angles they didn't want to go, and it tired us quickly. And they still kept coming!

Occasionally a small spot of open water appeared, never for more than 50 feet, and we would rejoice. But those were few and far between, and it was a long heavy battle to get up this stream. It was small enough to remain nameless on our maps so we dubbed it 'Alder Hell', a name that any who attempt it will find very appropriate.

To compound the frustration, we twice came upon larger trees that had fallen across our tiny stream. These barriers forced us to portage around them, and it was a struggle to force our way through all those alders with the canoe and gear, only to gain about five feet of progress each time.

After several hours of work, during which we made about a mile and a half of progress, we came up to a small pond. We were so happy! It was a quiet, circular body of water, no more than 100 yards across, and we quickly crossed it to find the entering stream on the other side. We climbed out and scouted along the thick, brushy, shore, finding this stream plagued with rocks and with no passable route up it. Option B was to portage around, but we didn't know how long the portage was, and there was no trail. This small pond maybe was Hull Pond, but then again, maybe wasn't, and so we opted to drag the canoe up again.

The stream will have the paint from our boat bottom for a long while yet. The rocks abounded, and the canoe groaned as we forced it up. Fortunately it was not too long before we arrived at another small body of water. This one was more of the shape of Hull Pond, and we thought, "At last, we've arrived! We're at the top of Alder Hell!"

The map said a faint trail led to Whipple Pond from Hull, but we couldn't find it, so we dragged up the small stream that led to Whipple, and there we were, at the top of the world! Whipple Pond was much bigger, and we paddled along the skinny part of it before coming out on a much larger open area. Across that was a clear portage sign. According to the map we would be heading due north along a dirt road. But when we got to the road, there was an arrow pointing due south. Shrugging our shoulders we turned south, but after walking a quarter mile with no change in direction we stopped. The map clearly said go due north, so we assumed the arrow was wrong, turned around, retraced our steps, and headed north, in direct opposition to what the sign said.

Almost immediately, we saw a moose and her calf. They stopped, looked at us for a second, and then ran off. In the distance we watched them walk along a ridge, outlined against the sky for us, before dropping down on the other side, out of sight. They were beautiful, and our moods skyrocketed. We walked about a mile north along the logging road, but the road quickly began to deteriorate, and after a mile it simply disappeared into the undergrowth. A faint game trail continued, and we dropped our gear before following it for another half mile. A pond appeared, but it certainly wasn't the Moose River, and I was almost certain that it was Boulder Pond. Very confused as to how Boulder Pond got there, since it was due north of Hull Pond and not Whipple (we hadn't made the connection yet), we returned to the gear, and re-carried the gear back to the original sign that pointed South. We had carried the gear a distance of about 2 ½ miles and walked an extra mile without it so far. Our frustration began to grow, and we decided to commit to following the sign, come hell or high water. So we picked up the gear and carried it ¾ mile south, with no further signs. Finally, we dropped our loads, and decided to scout ahead without the gear. We walked a further half mile with no loads, but the road still stayed south. Really pissed off now, we returned once again to the gear. The only thing I could think of was that the portage trail turned south at the sign, and then there was a quick left that we had somehow missed off the logging road. We carried our gear back, once again, to the offending sign, resolved to search nearby and see what else we could see. Otherwise we would bushwhack the mile from Boulder Pond to the Moose River, since that was all that we could think of to do. There was no question of returning via Alder Hell.

It was Andy who found it. A second sign, hidden behind the branches of a pine tree, pointed left up a stream populated by massive boulders. There was no trail, no marker, no nothing. Just the little sign nearly completely obscured by branches. We jumped, shouted, and screamed for joy and anger. We ran up the stream, hopping from boulder to boulder to arrive shortly at the true Whipple Pond, and realization dawned on us. Hull Pond was not Hull Pond but just some nothing open areas in the river. Whipple Pond was actually Hull Pond. And now we were looking out over the true Whipple Pond.

Filled with relief and happy to know where we were in the world, we returned to our gear on the logging road. It was already five o'clock so simply set up camp in the middle of the road. We covered only nine miles on the trail and walked a total of six useless miles, much of it with our gear. Feeling very tired, worn out, frustrated and most of all relieved we quickly ate dinner and went to bed under splattering rain.

Thank God Andy found the sign. Otherwise I had been contemplating bushwhacking a portage from the northern tip of the logging road to Moose River, which would have been several miles of hard work. Now we knew where we were, and we made a vow to put in a long, hard day tomorrow as well to make up for lost time.

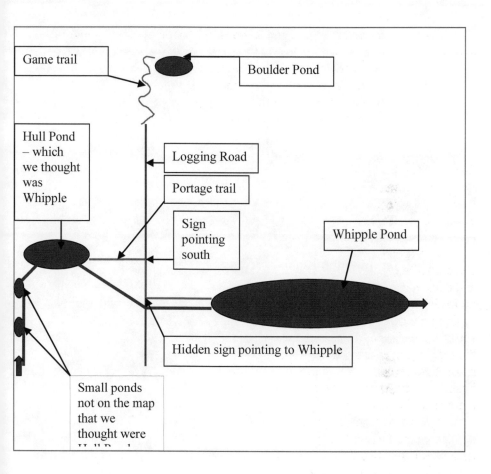

Game trail

Boulder Pond

Hull Pond – which we thought was Whipple

Logging Road

Portage trail

Sign pointing south

Whipple Pond

Hidden sign pointing to Whipple

Small ponds not on the map that we thought were

Hull Pond
– which we
thought
was
Whipple

Portage trail

Hidden sign pointing to Whipple

Hall Pond

Whipple

Logging Roads

Small ponds
not on the map
that we thought
were Hull Pond

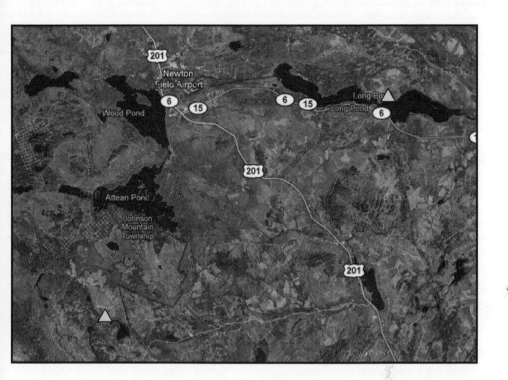

July 5th, Day 31 – Whipple Pond to Long Pond: We woke early in an effort to get an even greater jump on regaining ground. The remaining 200 yards of portage was up a stream, forcing us to hop from one rock to another while trying to simultaneously balance our gear and avoid slipping and falling into the water. The boulders were wet and mossy, and the footing poor. Our loads shifted around on us as we attempted to hop from boulder to boulder, with wannigans cutting into our skin and bags slipping off.

I loved it, and Andy loathed it.

I grew up hiking in the White Mountains of New Hampshire which often requires similar feats of balance. The Presidential Range especially is frequently made up of sharp jagged boulders piled on top of one another. I love to go skipping and running over the tops of them at full speed, challenging my feet to keep up with my body and protect me from bodily harm. Just one misstep could mean serious injury, but I don't misstep. Ever. I found it a joy to jump from one rock to another while trying to balance the canoe on my shoulders and not fall into the water. This short portage posed little trouble for me.

Andy was much more tentative about jumping over rocks with gear on his back. He picked his way carefully over rocks, hesitating before each step and taking his time. Because he took his time he would lean back against the angle of rocks, causing him to slip time and again, banging his shins and causing him to lean back even more. Andy hated every minute.

The real Whipple Pond was much nicer than Hull Pond, but it was also filled with boulders and we scraped a few barely submerged rocks as we crossed it. Both Hull and Whipple felt very wilderness-y. Besides the logging road there was no sign of human civilization, and we couldn't help but think that this is how the very first explorers and timber men found Maine when they arrived. The woods showed no sign of human passage in a long time, and there were certainly no sounds from humans either.

The ensuing portage into the Moose River was straightforward, and we were headed downstream again! For the rest of the trip!

Attean Falls was washed out because of all the rain so it was just fast-moving un-technical water. One rock at the bottom would have given us trouble but it was submerged enough that we cruised over it.

On Big Wood Pond we battled side winds coming from the west. Side winds can be very deadly since the canoe is forced to roll in an unnatural direction, but we had little choice. Water would slop over the side occasionally but we made it to Jackman without having to bail.

As we pulled into the beach at a small park, we watched a group of four canoes heading out for a day trip on the water. They were clearly novices and were struggling with the heavy winds. Switching sides frequently they still managed to make almost no headway and we chuckled at their struggles.

Lunch in town was a twelve-inch pastrami sub, a PB and J sandwich, and a bagel, egg, ham, and cheese sandwich, and I was still hungry. Canoeing sure builds up an appetite. We stopped at a yard sale to browse the selection but found nothing of value. The local hardware store provided us with some heavy duty wire to finally (so we thought) fix the bow seat which was only being held together by string and was threatening to break again. Then back on the water.

We went around a bend on Big Wood Pond, perhaps ½ mile from town, and we saw those same four canoes that we saw when we came into town! We had been on shore for nearly an hour and they had paddled barely ½ mile before we caught them. Poor novices!

We cruised down the Moose River, happy to be going with the flow. Low marshlands surrounded us and it was quite peaceful to simply be paddling gently along. Even when we got to Long Pond (one of two on our map and one of many on our trip – why can't people be more creative when naming bodies of water?) tailwinds pushed us on our way.

Conversation this afternoon centered on, not surprisingly, moose, and specifically the ill omens they seemed to be.

"Andy, do you know that the two times we've seen moose, we've gotten into map trouble?"

"What do you mean?"

"Well, first on the unnecessary mud portage between two islands on Flagstaff Lake. We saw a moose in the distance, remember? The second time was on the Whipple Pond portage debacle. We've seen moose twice, and only twice, and have gotten confused or lost twice, and only twice, and they've coincided both times!"

"So what are you saying? Moose are a curse on us? But I *like* moose. I *like* seeing them."

"Yup, and there are a lot of people who like flowers, but are still allergic to them. Do you see what I am saying, Andy? Beware the moose!"

"Sure Sam. Whatever."

Dinner tonight was burgers, cooked on the flattened out bean can. It did the trick and the bean-can burgers were delicious. As were the beans. Old cans, odd pieces of string, the odd wrench on the side of the road, every little thing was useful. Our mantra had become: "Throw nothing out. Everything has a purpose." Necessity is the mother of invention, as they say.

After dinner we sat on the shore and looked out over the lake, watching the sun set. It was cloudy for most of the day, but it was the first rain-less day we had had in Maine, and for that we were thankful. We went to bed pleased with the thirty miles we had accomplished, and ready for another big day to follow.

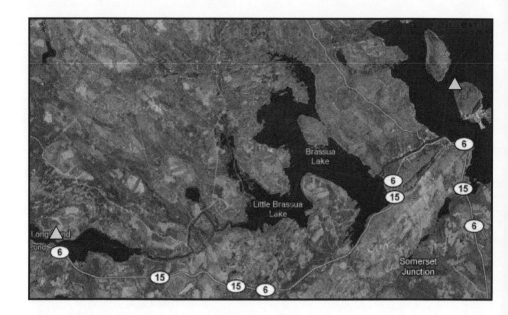

July 6th, Day 32 – Long Pond to Moosehead Lake: As I was making the fire to heat water for oatmeal and coffee, I heard a rustling nearby. I was crouched down over the small pile of twigs and birch bark I was about to light, and the shore was hidden from me by a small knoll, behind which I squatted. I stood to see what was making the noise, suspecting a chipmunk or squirrel, and to my surprise a bald eagle perched not ten feet in front of me! He was as surprised as I was because he immediately dropped the fish he was about to breakfast on and flapped away. He perched briefly in a tree, looked at me, at the fish again, then at me, and then took off for good. Whether he was estimating distances in an effort to retrieve his meal or he was making sure that I understood the proffered fish was a token of goodwill and harmony, I'll never know, but he left it. The event did indeed usher in the first sunny day we had in Maine.

Leaving the fish in case he returned – we weren't hungry for fish that morning – we paddled the remainder of Long Pond and hit the Moose again. The river was significantly bigger here and we were forced to take out at a bridge at Demo Road before the river got too fierce.

As I began to walk along Demo Road, a moose crossed the dusty expanse far in front of me. Uh-oh. It was just yesterday we had discovered "The Curse of the Moose". I took my map out of my pocket and double-checked it. Yes, I was on the correct road (the only road just about): "Take the second right onto an old logging road just before Demo Brook crosses Demo Road." I turned down the second dirt road, just as the map showed and walked to the end of an old logging road. I could hear the river in front of me, perhaps 200 yards away, but no path to it. I put the canoe down and searched up and down the dirt road, looking for any sign of a path. Nothing. Andy arrived and we both searched. Nothing.

"The hell with it, Andy. Let's 'shwack it."

"I don't know, Sam. Maybe we turned down the wrong dirt road…"

Andy was always the voice of reason. I would just get bull-headed and want to continue to forge ahead come hell or high water. Unfortunately, I once again prevailed and we decided to bushwhack it.

It was only about 200 yards to the river, but it was through swampy, low-lying brush and it was a battle to force the canoe through groves of alders. We managed with much effort, cursing, and scratches, only to find ourselves on top of a steep embankment dropping thirty feet to the river. We managed that as well, the canoe being held back by only my neck as we descended steeply. A new argument presented itself.

"Sam, we should paddle downstream until we find the take-out at the bottom of this set of rapids, where we are supposed to be. Then we can retrace the real trail and find out where we went wrong."

"Nu-uh. What if we don't find anything? Then we are up a creek without a paddle, so to speak. We should bushwhack all the gear to this place, then continue on."

Andy won out, against my better judgment, and sure enough around two more bends we found the true end to the portage, followed the trail back to the road, and found our way. Why I didn't listen to Andy in all questions of importance I'll never know.

This time the map was at fault, not us. The logging road we were supposed to turn down was *after* Demo Brook, not before as the map showed. The moose had warned us, and we had failed to listen. "The Curse of the Moose" lived on!

The rest of the day was perfect. We paddled across a picture-perfect lake with sun in the sky, white fluffy clouds overhead, loons calling, and a stiff breeze going our way. It was an extremely pleasant afternoon and our spirits were sky-high. These kinds of days were why we came on the trip. Life couldn't have been better.

A short portage later and we made it to Moosehead Lake. We camped under the shadow of Mount Kineo, one of the world's largest deposits of volcanic rhyolite (although what one might use rhyolite for I have no idea).

As we turned in for the night it began to rain again. So much for a rainless day. At least we got some sun in. The string of one rain-less day ended, and it would be back to rain for the next couple days. We took what came, since we didn't have much other choice.

Chapter 9: West Branch Penobscot River and the Headwaters of the Allagash

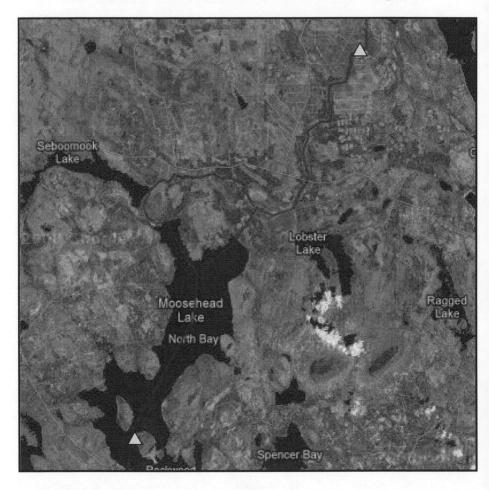

July 5th, Day 33 – Moosehead Lake to West Branch Penobscot River: We battled headwinds and rain all morning as we made our way northwards on Maine's largest lake. It was tough work and we silently hunkered down and simply paddled hard all morning, trying to keep the water from trickling down our backs and soaking us. We failed miserably and were quite wet by the day's end.

Northeast Carry, a well-known route used by Indians for hundreds of years as well as Henry David Thoreau when he traveled the area, was now a dirt road and we portaged easily along it, stopping at a small general store near the southern end.

Ed Raymond has been running Raymond's Country Store for nearly thirty years. Previously, he worked for Texas Instruments but when he found himself in a dead-end job he didn't like, he lit out for the woods. He and his wife (gone for the day) have been here, in the middle of nowhere, ever since.

"But the government is still trying to stick it to us," he said. "Do you know I need to have more than thirty licenses to run this place? I need a liquor license, a fresh food license, a gas license, a tobacco license; I need all sorts of licenses. I need a processed meat license, for Christ's sake, because I sell Slim Jims. Slim Jims! I probably lose more money than I make on Slim Jim's, because of the god damn licenses."

He told us how he had kicked a state inspector out of his store when the inspector became impertinent with him.

"They had been sending the same old inspector year after year, and we had an understanding. We got along fine. He knew me, knew I ran a tight store, and he let me be. Well one year, they send a new guy up, and he starts getting snippy with me and my wife. He was trying to tell me I need to use a four decimal-place scale to weigh my meat. I told him nobody freaking cares about that many decimal places. You know what he does? He tells me he is going to fine me the big bucks, and drive me out of business for not abiding by the law. Huh! Well I told him I could take him out, bury him in the backyard, and even if the neighbors found out, they wouldn't rat me out. And they wouldn't! They know I'm a stand-up guy, and that I won't stand for none of this. So I told this new inspector that I'd bury him, and never get caught. He goes and insults my wife and myself, in my place of business! And my home! So I kicked him out. I told him to send the other guy. Well he goes back to his superiors, and they send the old guy. And he apologizes! That old guy knew how to treat a business owner. These new guys, I just don't know. It's hard enough trying to run a business without being harassed by the government."

But he was very friendly to us, frying us several cheeseburgers and telling us about the moose hunting nearby. He even offered to portage our gear for free to the other end of the portage with his truck. We declined and his surprise was evident. He too was doubtful about the feasibility of wannigans.

"Don't knock them until you try them," Andy told him.

Paddling on the West Branch of the Penobscot River was a pleasure. Clouds still hung low over us and the afternoon was dreary, but at least it wasn't raining.

We passed a camp group, stopped at Thoreau Island, who watched us as we floated by. One kid shouted out, "Are you paddling the Northern Forest Canoe Trail?"

Our affirmative resulted in a rousing round of applause from the group and we went on, warmed by the cheer.

Thoreau came through here in the 1840's and '50s, paddling his canoe along the Penobscot and other rivers. We retraced part of his journey in our own boat, but it must have been a completely different world that he saw. Instead of established campsites, groups of school kids, and occasional bridges, he found just an empty wilderness. Using local guides to help him on his way, he was one of the first people to chronicle Maine's North Woods and his book, <u>The Maine Woods</u>, remains one of the first glimpses into Maine's untouched wilderness, pre-logging era (Thoreau 1950). The woods remained "stern and savage," as Thoreau once found them, and we paddled through some of the last remaining wilderness areas in the Eastern United States on the NFCT.

Dinner was hot dogs and beans and we ad-libbed an ode to our final meal of franks as we ate:

O hot dogs,
I love you more than life itself.
To my taste,
There is nothing else.

And beans, sweet beans,
You are so good.
And now to bed,
My stomach full of food.

Poets, we were not.

The night turned cold and we kept the fire going for warmth, the first night we chose to do so. I was thankful I had brought a warm coat.

We sat around the dying fire, watching embers smolder and throwing in the occasional twig, when Andy let out a sudden, "O Jesus Lord!" A bird had landed on his head, mistaking it for a branch. We chuckled over the incident before finally letting the fire die and turning in for the night.

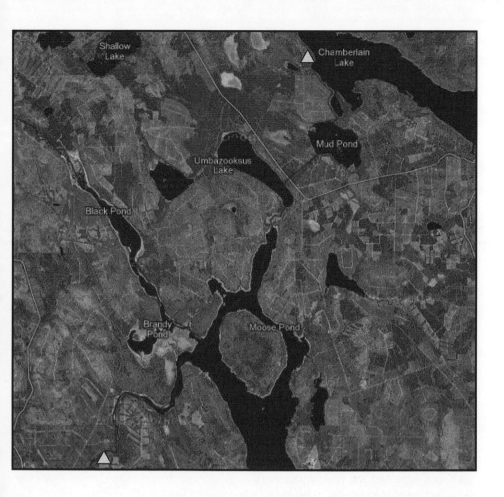

July 8th, Day 34 – West Branch Penobscot River to Chamberlain Lake: The last six miles (for our trip) on the Penobscot were gentle and we paddled quickly down them in the rain (of course), stopping in at Chesuncook Village.

Chesuncook Village was a tiny village, not much more than a small cluster of buildings. A few small summer houses dotted the woods and shore. There was a small church where a visiting pastor resides each summer, giving sermons on Sundays. Other than that there was very little. Dirt paths connected the few buildings around, and we saw no one about. Paths meandered through the woods from one house to another, and it felt as though we'd slipped back in time a century or two.

We walked through town, stopping in at "The Store". A metal bell hung outside which we rang, and a thin man in stained jeans stepped out.

"Come on in. You here for some cookies?" "The Store" sells only cookies, fudge, and homemade root beer, but it is a well-known paddler destination in the area, and Andy had stopped years before on a canoe trip with his summer camp.

We entered and sat down in plastic lawn chairs on the walled-in porch, introducing ourselves to Bill. I immediately asked about "The Store."

"Well, this isn't really my store. I'm filling in for Jack who has been running it for years. He is feeling poorly these days so I stop in and help out."

We ordered cookies, fudge, and root beer floats, which were all delicious. Bill was shy and didn't say much, so Andy and I worked at making conversation. Living in such a quiet place in the middle of northern Maine must have curbed his enthusiasm for chatter.

"So do you live in town?" Andy asked.

"Yup. I'm sort of the village handyman, so I keep folks' houses in good repair when they aren't around. These are mostly summer houses so I keep an eye on them, make sure they aren't falling apart, and help close and open them in the fall and spring."

I was curious about the chapel.

"Do you have a full time pastor here?"

"No. It's a visiting pastor – a new one each week. We get some pretty good ones and most everyone who is here goes each Sunday. Anybody who is willing to spend a week in the woods, use an outhouse, etc. is usually a pretty good person and a pretty good pastor, so we have some excellent sermons."

"Yeah, I suppose that's a good way to be naturally selective about your pastors…" I'm not much of a church-goer but it made sense to me.

"Well these cookies sure are delicious. Thanks!" Freshly baked goods had never tasted so good.

"These are actually my second batch of the morning. I'm still learning to bake, and I burned the first batch. I'm actually trying to get rid of them. You two wouldn't want burnt cookies by any chance would you?"

Andy and I looked at each other, then back at Bill nodding simultaneously and enthusiastically. When he brought them out they were only slightly crisped around the edges. We took four each, and profusely thanking him, headed back on our way.

"Andy, could you live in a town like this, with nothing going on?"

"You know, I don't think so. I need a little more going on around me than here. It's just too quiet. I wouldn't know what to do with all my time. You?"

"Maybe. It certainly would be peaceful." And maybe I could. It looked kind of depressing in the rain, but I thought it certainly would be possible to live there. There certainly wouldn't be a whole lot to worry about, and I could hike, paddle, read, and relax. Perhaps just for a summer. At some point I would have to go out and see some more of the world. Bill appeared to be happy there, and as we left him in Chesuncook I couldn't help but be a little jealous.

We paddled up a small stream (fifteen minutes so it didn't even really count as upstream) into Umbazooskus Lake, worrying about the coming portage.

We'd been talking about it off and on for the past week, and Andy in particular was afraid it didn't exist.

"If I remember, all the blogs and notes I read prior to the trip, most people skipped this part, or got rides around it. I read only one where the people actually went on it, and they said it was a bushwhack portage."

Studying the map, we saw it was almost two miles. No matter what kind of undergrowth exists, even if it's clear beneath the trees, a bushwhack portage by compass through unknown terrain for two miles is not something to be trifled with. We entered Umbazooskus Lake with trepidation. The previous night we had talked it over and committed to doing it, no matter what. We wanted to do every inch of the Trail, and no bushwhack portage was going to stop us. But it was probably going to be Hell.

We paddled along the northeast shore until we got to the approximate spot on the map where it appeared the portage led off to the northeast. Paddling slowly along the shore we saw nothing. Lots of alders blocked the way, the trees looked thick and we could tell this was going to be ugly. But we were hard set upon doing it.

When we got past where we thought the portage was supposed to be, we stopped and unloaded the gear onto the small rocky shore. Alders and nearly impassable underbrush loomed in front of us.

"I guess here is as good as anywhere, right?"

"I guess. Do you think it thins out past these initial low trees?"

"I hope so. It's tough to tell. How long do you reckon it'll take us?"

"I don't know, five or six hours, perhaps. Maybe more. These bushes look thick. We should stick together through this whole thing. Do you have your compass?"

Andy got it out, and studied it.

"Northeast is almost along the shore here. Wait a second! We must not be far enough along the shore, because on the map northeast points almost perpendicularly away from the water, and here, it's almost parallel with the shore!"

I checked my map.

"You're right. Do you think we should have paddled further along?"

"Yes I do. Let's leave the gear here. Remember the blog said it was a bushwhack portage so don't get your hopes up. But let's take a paddle and see what we can find."

And Voila! Perhaps another quarter mile further down the shore we found two tall cairns of rocks and a pink ribbon fluttering from a tree marking the beginning of the portage! We breathed a huge sigh of relief, thanked all the gods we could think of, and returned for the gear.

The portage was far from pretty however. The path was a dirt track that was sunk perhaps one foot below the surrounding land from erosion. It was straight as an arrow and nigh impossible to get lost on, but it was definitely a rarely used trail. Since we had had nothing but rain for the last week, the track was filled to the brim with water, and we sloshed, stumbled, and tripped for two miles as we caught our feet on submerged roots and rocks. Curses rent the air occasionally, and by the end we were dog-tired, soaked and muddy.

"Thank God we found the trail," Andy commented, and I couldn't agree more. Trying to bushwhack that by compass would truly have been Hell.

We set up camp on Chamberlain Lake and ate a "smitches and dabs" dinner of stovetop stuffing, mashed potatoes, rice, pasta, and canned beef stew all in one pot, which was delicious. The sky began to clear as we finished the dishes and we rested under clear blue skies looking out over the lake afterwards.

It was right near our campsite that in 1880 Thomas S. Steele, outdoor enthusiast and author, and his friend "Colonel G." startled a bull caribou that fled before they could level their rifles. They had just started a 400-mile canoe trip of their own, beginning in Moosehead Lake and following our route (or rather we were following their route) to Eagle Lake before heading east while we continued north. Colonel G.'s frustrated exclamation, as quoted by Mr. Steele, at the loss of such a valuable meal is worth repeating for posterity: "Exceedingly impolite of the beast to decamp so suddenly – he would have weighed three hundred pounds if an ounce!" (Steele 1882) Sometimes I can't help but wish that people still spoke in such a manner. The world would perhaps have a more refined sense of humor.

As we settled down to enjoy the evening, swatting the occasional bug, Andy asked, "Do you suppose that there are two guys who feel as though they've accomplished as much today as we have, and feel as thankful for that trail, rough though it was, as we do?" I didn't think so (Mr. Steele and his friend the Colonel portaged this section by wagon, so even they did not achieve the level of satisfaction we felt.)

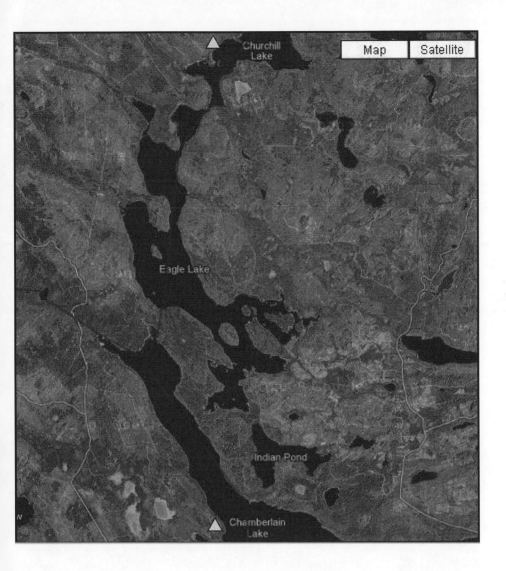

July 9th, Day 35 – Chamberlain Lake to Churchill Lake: I was up before Andy as always, but I had company. A rabbit was hopping around the cleared area of the campsite, munching on grass. With each hop he got closer to me until he was about ten feet away, eating his breakfast while I ate mine. He would take a big chomp of his grass, stare at me for half a beat, take another chomp, and stare again. You could almost hear his teeth coming together with each bite, and he was clearly hinting, "Give me food!" He must be the local camp rabbit, half tame, who lives off of camper scraps. To quote Ed Raymond of Raymond's General Store, "rabbits are just fodder, meant to be eaten by anyone and everyone." If this rabbit wasn't careful, then he is likely to end up as breakfast himself.

Our first couple strokes on the lake and we became immersed in fog. The shore, just a few dozen feet behind us, quickly disappeared and we felt as though we were floating in space. Only a ten foot radius of water was visible around the canoe, and we seemed to exist in a vacuum, where nothing else lived and nothing else mattered. Our strokes were muted by the mist, and we remained silent, as though any sound would break the spell.

As the sun began to rise, however, a bright orb entered our world, rising slowly to our right. Our circle began to expand as the mist burnt off, and as the day continued, the spell broke. Shore, trees, sky, and the rest of the world again entered our consciousness and we were faced with the fact that something else existed besides just ourselves and our boat. But for a moment, we were the only things on earth, alone in a small globe of fog.

On the east shore of Chamberlain Lake (named for Joshua Chamberlain, the famed Civil War general and professor at Bowdoin College who was integral to the Union victory at Gettysburg) we found the rusting remains of an old log-boom towboat which was retired in the early 1900's, a powerful monument to the logging era of Maine (Northern Forest Canoe Trail 2005).

The portage into Eagle Lake was even more amazing. On the Chamberlain Lake side of the portage rests the rusting remnants of a diesel engine which ran a "log tramway" between Chamberlain and Eagle Lakes. Along the portage parts of the remains of the conveyor belt and tramway could be seen, and at the far side rested two massive locomotives. They were slightly rusted but otherwise were in great condition. A small plaque at their base told us they were used for only seven years, running thirteen miles from Eagle Lake to Umbazooksus Lake. Logs were then dumped into the lake and floated down the Penobscot River. The trains ran day and night, stopping only to be serviced when needed. Although they only ran from 1927 to 1933, they were hugely profitable, in spite of the massive costs required to bring the locomotives, track, facilities, and equipment deep into the Maine Woods. A 1,800 foot railroad trestle was even built across part of Chamberlain Lake. It hauled 7,500 cords of wood a week when in operation. However, in 1933 the wood of the region had been exploited and the locomotives backed into their depot for the last time. Sometime in the 1970's the shed burned down, but the Forest Service righted the tipping locomotives and they stand on the same location today, exposed to the weather, a proud testament to the glory days of logging in Maine (Parker 1996).

Just past the two engines, set in a clearing, we crossed the tracks that the trains ran on. Stretching into the woods to the east were the box cars that the engines pulled. Their undercarriages still rested on the tracks though much of the wooden box cars had rotted and collapsed. After dropping our gear we followed the tracks into the woods, and they just kept going. Trees had grown up in between the tracks and the forest was mostly returned to its pristine state but the tracks remain as a testament to a long ago day when there was lots of money to be made in this area. The sheer immensity of the project was overawing and we were mightily impressed that an operation this large, running for such a short time, was as successful as it was.

We camped on Churchill Lake, now officially on the Allagash Wilderness Waterway. The Allagash Wilderness Waterway was established in 1966 when the state of Maine purchased a strip of land 500 feet in width surrounding the Allagash River, eventually creating the Allagash Wilderness Waterway. In 1970 it became the first designated state-administered wild river in the National Wild and Scenic Rivers System. It represents approximately 100 miles of wild river and is one of the last remaining wilderness areas in the northeast with few roads, camps or developments (Northern Forest Canoe Trail 2005).

Next to us was a noisy summer camp. They had balls, toys, hammocks, and tons of food so we were surprised when their counselors told us they were out for 16 days. Thankfully they quieted down after dinner, and camped a little ways away from us so they weren't too bothersome. The noise and fervor of twenty adolescents running around was a bit of a shock to us who had only had each other for company for the past month.

Chapter 10: The Allagash and St. John Rivers

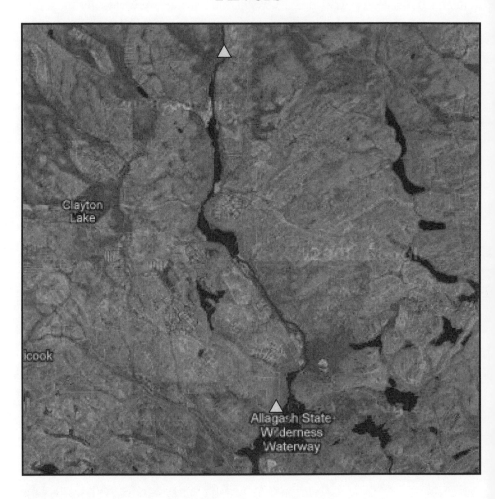

July 10th, Day 36 – Churchill Lake to Cunliffe Island on the Allagash River:
We paddled out across the lake leaving the (thankfully) still slumbering camp behind, pausing only to wave a silent farewell to the one staff man who was awake. Two moose also stood vigil on the shore nearby, snacking on watery vegetation.

"You don't suppose these moose are another warning, do you?" I asked.

"Nahh. We're on the water today. Moose are only bad omens on the portage trail."

I nodded thankfully. We took moose very seriously after our first three encounters, so it was good to know that these moose were of the benevolent variety. It held true for the remainder of the moose we saw on the water; they bore no ill will, simply willing us onwards with their very presence.

At the end of Churchill Lake stands Churchill Dam and a ranger station which monitors the dam releases each morning to make Chase Rapids runnable. Tradition holds that you pay a couple of bucks to have the ranger shuttle your gear via truck around the top sets while you run empty boats. When we arrived at the dam, however, two large groups were already waiting to have their gear shuttled, and we would have had to wait at least forty five minutes. We stopped briefly, talking to one extremely unorganized group with gear scattered *all* over the place.

"You guys setting up shop here?"

One guy took a long drag of his cigarette – they all were smoking – and grinned. "Nope. Those two idiots," – pointing – "over there wrapped a boat on Chase Rapids yesterday, and snapped two thwarts. Tough to believe I know. We're waiting for the shuttle to take the gear, then we will try to run 'em again."

The two idiots laughed, and the shaggier-looking one spoke up, "This is our first time in whitewater, and we got into a tight spot. Better luck today I hope!"

They asked us about our route, and upon telling them we had paddled from New York they asked, "Aren't you tired?"

Andy and I looked at each other and laughed. Andy responded, "Well, we did sleep each night. It's not like we've been paddling straight through. Besides, we're outside, working hard, eating well, and are very active. We're in fantastic shape and are probably the best rested and most content we've been in a long time." And it was true. We were the opposite of tired. We were happy and at peace. Tired? Far from it!

Pausing only briefly to make a call to Andy's mother to arrange a pick-up time in Fort Kent, we continued on our way since we were uninterested in waiting for the shuttle on a dusty road. We portaged the short 100 yards around the dam and continued on our way.

Chase Rapids were quite bony even with the dam release and we kept up a running dialogue of "Alright, moving to left center here, just to the right of the pointy rock, hitting this "V" here…okay good now moving right into the main current…good…just left of this pillow, through these waves…good…etc."

I, in particular, preferred to always be talking, letting Andy know what I was thinking, where I was going, why I was steering the boat the way I was. This way everyone was on the same page and no one was working against each other.

We bumped over some rocks in the shallow water but had no serious trouble and came out onto Umsaskis Lake before long. The sun was burning very brightly and we swam in the lake during our lunch stop before slathering on sunscreen. Lunch was on a rocky peninsula and we sunbathed with water on three sides, looking out over the blue of the lake stirred by gentle breezes, the green of the forest startling in its contrast, and the lighter blue of the sky marred only by a few wispy clouds. It was stunning.

The afternoon was spent lazily paddling up Long Lake (yes, *another* "Long" body of water) before returning to the Allagash and camping on Cunliffe Island. Four more moose watched us pass, clearly inured to paddlers.

We set up camp before lazing around in the shade for a late afternoon rest hour. As I sat on the bank of the river, a moose wandered along the far shore, perhaps 75 feet away. He did much the same routine as the bunny on Chamberlain Lake: munching on grass while staring at us before taking a few steps nearer. Perhaps he was as curious and enthralled by us as we are by him, but I doubted it. He, unlike the rabbit, had nothing to fear in these woods since wolves disappeared long ago and hunters are not permitted along the Allagash so he wanders at will. Andy and I sat silently and watched him for half an hour before he moved on about his business.

Ducks swam by in families. The young ones are much larger than those we saw at the beginning of the trip and it was nice to see them growing up. Later, as we cooked dinner, a Mama rabbit and three of her brood hopped up, attracted by the scent perhaps. They were playful, hopping close by before sprinting into the woods, only to return again.

"Rabbit stew would taste right nice about now," I told Andy. Perhaps the rabbits understood my looks at them because they took one final glance before bounding off for good.

Dinner was canned ham – better than it sounds once we had grilled it and put canned pineapple on top. Then we went to bed under the brilliant Maine stars, thankful for a cloudless, rainless evening.

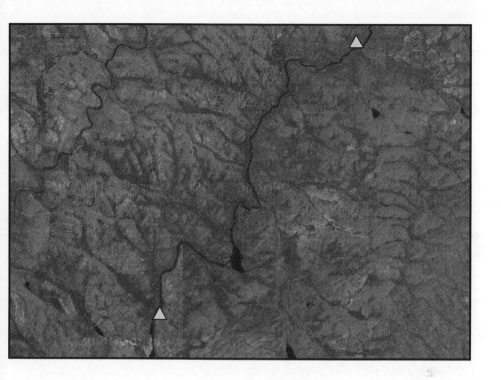

July 11ᵗʰ – Day 37 – Cunliffe Island to Allagash Falls: Morning holds so much potential. There is a coolness and crispness in the air that evenings lack, a sense of alertness in the awakening world. The river gurgles past, somehow more cheerfully and energetically than the evening before. Animals stir and birds begin their morning serenade. The chance and opportunity that the new day holds seems to invigorate everything around.

Early into the day's paddle we passed under one of the few bridges that cross the Allagash. The sun was already hot and we decided to jump. A quick check with our paddles found the river bottom to be at least six feet below the surface and since the bridge was only fifteen feet high, we figured we were safe. It turns out the river was only seven or eight feet deep so we hit bottom relatively hard. No injuries, however, and we laughingly continued on our way, vowing to check a little better next time.

We passed a group of three boats poling upriver. I was very impressed and asked where they were headed. "To Chamberlain!" they responded. We passed them in a flat but flowing section of the river so while they were moving slowly, they were making steady progress. I imagine they had a tougher time in the whitewater. It was quite an undertaking, however. Not too many folks go *up* the Allagash.

We stopped for lunch next to a ranger cleaning a campsite. After introducing ourselves, we asked her about her work.

"I'm stationed at Round Pond, and I keep an eye on the surrounding campsites and interact with any paddlers coming through. It's a fantastic job, but it's also really competitive. There are a ton of folks who would love to be out here, so I'm lucky to have it. This is my third year, and I love it."

"What exactly would we have to do to get the job?" As seniors in college, we were very interested.

"Well I have a degree in Parks and Recreation, which helps a lot. Experience in this kind of a thing is very helpful as well. But keep an eye out online. All these jobs are posted at the U.S. government site."

We thanked her profusely and continued on our way, dreaming of living on the Allagash Wilderness Waterway all summer long. It would be quite a way to spend three months: living and working in one of the most beautiful regions in Maine, away from just about everything.

We checked out of the AWW at Michaud Farm, chatting with the ranger there about the high water, high volume of people on the river, and the potential for hail that night. She also told us that she had seen a mountain lion several years ago crossing the river, which we were very dubious of. A poster on her wall stated that mountain lions were no longer found in the wild, but she was insistent and a little research uncovers dozens of supposed sightings annually of big cats. There is no photographic evidence, but even the Maine Department of Environmental Protection's website leaves the question open, waiting for concrete evidence. Who knows? All we could say for sure was that they didn't show their faces to us, though we kept an eye out after this conversation.

We camped along the portage trail around Allagash Falls, swimming and taking pictures. We arrived at 2:30 although we had covered almost 30 miles on the day, so we had lots of time on our hands.

Soon after we arrived, however, several families of locals came trotting up the trail from downstream and all piled into the campsite right next to ours. One of the fathers came over, introduced himself as Mitch and invited us over to their fire for hot dogs and beer in a thick Maine accent. We grinned and happily accepted, plopping ourselves down among five or six young kids, a guy and girl our own age, and five or six older parents.

"How you doing there?" Mitch asked. "Have some dogs – good red Maine hot dogs. You know a true Maine hot dog when it's red. The red is because the casing is natural. Or some beer? Have some beer, I'll bet you're thirsty."

The stream of chatter didn't stop. They incessantly poked fun at each other and had a fantastic time. We managed to get out of them that they were only up here for the afternoon, cooking out and enjoying the Falls, before they would motorboat back home to St. Francis and St. John.

The one particular butt of many of their jokes was the guy, John, our age, who was there as the boyfriend of Mitch's daughter. He had driven one of the motorboats up here, but in the process had been swigging too many beers so by the time he reached the campsite he was quite drunk. Just before arrival he had managed to get his boat stuck on a rock, something that is tough to do in a motorboat with an engine. The others were kidding him incessantly, but he was too inebriated to adequately defend himself and he mostly just sat there smiling drunkenly. His girlfriend got some ribbing as well of the "Just exactly what do you see in this guy?" variety.

Mitch was hilarious. He was slightly overweight and had the sort of guileless face that asks to be made fun of. His thick Maine accent helped not at all, and everyone clearly thought Mitch was a hoot. He presided over the crew, but was so good-natured and humorous that no one could take him seriously.

Andy and I didn't have to do much at all. We just sat there, enjoying ourselves and the conversations flowing around us. As soon as we finished a hot dog another would be proffered, along with another beer. Wine began to flow out of a bag as well.

Mitch embarked on a fish story, clearly embellished, as he was cooking a hot dog. He got so excited in the telling of it that when he finished and finally checked his hot dog, he found only a burning stick, the hot dog charred into a nearly-unrecognizable state in the fire. In a thick accent, he announced, "Whoops, I just lost my hot dog," staring mournfully at his hot-dog-less stick and the group fell about the place in hilarity.

They left around six much to our dismay since they were such a lively and cheerful bunch. Their generosity and good humor were infective and we went to bed that night in fantastic moods, perhaps partially because we were both more than a little drunk as well.

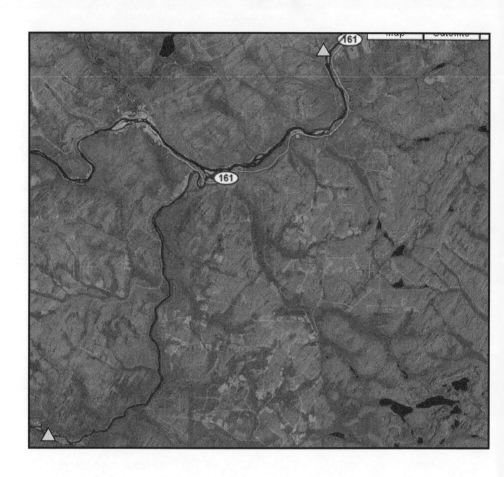

July 12th, Day 38 – Allagash Falls to the St. John River: We woke up to blue skies although it rained pretty heavily overnight. Throughout the morning we waved at other paddlers still breaking camp along the river as we paddled by – we were clearly the early risers for the day. We passed McGargle Rocks, a small riff named for a log driver who lost his life trying to clear a log jam, and Ghost Landing Bar named for another logger killed by a falling tree who supposedly haunts the area (Northern Forest Canoe Trail 2005). It was too nice a morning for ghosts to be about, however, so we weren't worried about any specters.

Lunch was at a dinner in the town of Allagash right along the river where we ate the Moosetown Special which included sausage, bacon, home fries, eggs, toast, donuts, pancakes and coffee. It was delicious and we played our final matches of checkers for the trip, Andy taking the cake two games to one. Afterwards we wandered up and down route 161 through town, finding very little of interest. We kept an eye out for Mitch and company but they were not in sight.

That afternoon we drifted much of the way down the river. Andy smoked a cigar he had bought to celebrate the end of the trip, but celebration was not really the mood of the day. We remained largely silent. I dipped a paddle occasionally to steer the boat and keep it in the current but besides that we remained still and spoke little. The sun shone down on us and we enjoyed its warmth, the sound of the river moving past us, and the creak of the boat if we shifted our weight, but it was a quiet enjoyment. The trip was coming to an end, in a few hours we would be at our final campsite, and the mood was more melancholy than celebratory.

We planned to camp at a campsite near Golden Rapids, but it didn't seem to exist so we continued further downstream, searching vainly for a bush campsite out of sight of the road which skirted river right. We finally found a spot just past Rankin Rapids, back in the trees with some privacy.

For dinner we cleaned out the wannigans, eating whatever was left. As we picked up our pot from the fire the rubber handle came off, melted from the fire. Fortunately we only had breakfast the next morning, so it wasn't a big deal.

There is a real longing for civilization as a wilderness journey ends. A push for civilization. You yearn for cars, food, bars, and people. But almost as soon as you finish, you yearn to be back in the bush. Perhaps that is what the voyageurs of old felt too, or cowboys, or miners. They would all gear up for town, make a big to-do about it, and talk about it for much of the weeks leading up to it. But when they hit town, they'd blow all their money as quickly as they could and be back out on the trail, in the woods, at their claims quickly. Perhaps a subconscious something telling them they belong in the woods. Such it will be for us. For the last several days we've been looking forward to the end, to that last paddle stroke. But as soon as our bow hits the beach for the final time, we will be longing to be out in the woods again.

The contrast is the important thing: we wouldn't value the woods as much as we do if we didn't have civilization. Joy is only true joy if you've known sadness as well.

We sat around the fire until it got dark, thinking bittersweet thoughts, before hitting the hay once the last rays of sun dipped below the horizon. Nothing remained to be said. We would miss these nights, these days on the water. But all good things must come to an end and we fell asleep pleased with all that we had accomplished, wishing only that it could go on.

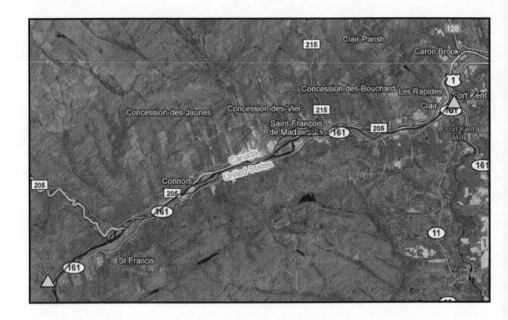

July 13ᵗʰ, Day 39 – The St. John River to Fort Kent, Maine: The remaining twenty miles of river were gentle. The St. John opened up, spreading its waters across sand and gravel bars. Birds shrieked in the bright morning air. Maine started with rain but it ended with some truly stunning days. We paddled steadily but easily, talking about the first things we would eat when we got home.

"I always crave donuts. Good cider donuts. I had them in Plattsburgh, and I want some more. Homemade, off a farm, drenched in cinnamon sugar. Mmmm."

Andy shook his head. "What I really want is a good steak. Not these two buck steaks we've been eating, but a good filet mignon, marinated for hours in some sauce, any sort of sauce. And –"

I cut him off. "Or blueberry pie. With ice cream. And a chocolate shake."

"And some real mashed potatoes. I know we've been eating mashed potatoes out here, but I want real ones, not just potato flakes. With butter. And sour cream. O God."

We meandered around the bends, drawing ever closer to the end of our trip, saliva nearly dripping from the roofs of our mouths. Canada to our left, the United States to our right, and us, caught in the middle, heading inexorably to the end of our trip, to our goal's finish.

I thought about all the people I hadn't seen in a month and a half. It would be great to catch up with my family: Dad and my brothers, my step-mom and step-sisters. It felt like it had been ages since I had last seen them and I couldn't help but think about all the things they had done with their summers as well.

I thought about Elizabeth as well. It had been a month since we had spent the zero day at her house, and I was really looking forward to her pretty face again as well. I felt confident that she was someone that I wanted to spend some more time with, not only because she understood my need for this trip, and other trips, but because she is a great person. As they say, absence makes the heart grow fonder, and in this case it was true. I couldn't wait to see her.

We wound in and out of small islands, letting the current direct which channel we would take. It didn't matter so much. They all led to Fort Kent, to the end.

Yet it didn't feel like the end. This trip, like so many, was more about the journey than about the finish. We had discovered so much over the past weeks about each other and about ourselves. We had traveled through nearly all of the wilderness areas that New England has left to offer. We learned about much of the small town history that inundates the countryside and rivers of the region. And we had become more comfortable with ourselves, as people. We knew we could accomplish things that only months before appeared to be up in the air. We had found our way when lost, had battled bugs, rain and lost gear. We had watched the sunset and the sunrise across New England. We had endured "the curse of the moose" and long portages. Most of all, we had overcome all obstacles in our path and continued onwards, remaining in good spirits, to persist to the end of the trail and successfully complete the challenge we had set for ourselves.

For me, that was what it was all about. Set a challenge, prepare for it, go out and do it, and overcome it. I love being outside, in the woods, doing things that few people have done before me. The tranquility, serenity, and peace that the outdoors fills me with is a high that I can find nowhere else. This journey reaffirmed this for me, and made me more than ever committed to working in and protecting the natural world. Too much of what humans do degrades the environment, and for Andy and me to be able to embrace it, if only for s short time before returning to school, work, family and life, is a treasure.

Our paddle strokes slowed as we neared Fort Kent. We passed under a large bridge, surprisingly unmarked on our map, before hugging the right shore and looking for Fish Island. Paddling along, Andy spotted a boat landing on the right and, thinking perhaps we had passed Fish Island, we pulled in to get our bearings. There stood the Northern Forest Canoe Trail's Eastern Terminus kiosk. We were done.

It came so suddenly, we weren't sure what to do. We slowly got to our feet and stretched on shore. We took pictures of each other in front of the kiosk, and strutted about like peacocks. But no one was around to witness the event, and so we returned to the canoe and began to unload the gear, piling it on the shore.

"Well Andy, thanks for coming. I had a good time. We didn't do too badly, eh?"

"No, I guess not. No, I'd say we did a pretty fine job, at that. You suppose there's anything to eat in this town?"

"Well, we can rustle up something, I'm sure. Anything will be better than our own cooking." I paused then said, "I guess we're done paddling for a while."

Andy shook his head. "I guess so. Hey, Sam?"

"Yes Andy?"

"We should do this again, sometime. Not this Trail, I mean. Some other trail. I mean, this was fun. We're a pretty good team, you know? So we should do this again."

"That'd be great Andy. I agree, we should do this again."

Turning the canoe over on top of the gear to shelter it from the drizzle, we walked into town. We grabbed a quick bite to eat at a local diner then returned to the boat launch where we found Andy's mother waiting. The gear was loaded up in no time and before we knew it, we were on our way, heading south towards the cities and back to "real life."

Post Script

Paddling the Northern Forest Canoe Trail was an amazing journey. Not only would I encourage each and every person to go out and paddle, if not the whole thing, at least a couple days or even a couple miles of it. No other Trail has linked the waterways, communities, and history in such an effective and unified manner. Every stroke taken held some sort of history and we could almost feel the ghosts of past travelers and explorers disappearing around the bend in front of us. As we followed in the paddle strokes of countless other outdoors enthusiasts, we couldn't help but feel that we were a small part of a much bigger picture, spread out across time and space. It was a truly amazing journey and I know that no other experience will be quite like it.

I will continue, however, to indulge in my love for the outdoors. Living my life any other way would be going against my very genetic make-up. Something out there calls my name and around every corner holds new mystery, wonder and beauty. I can't resist it and so whenever I can, I shall go a-tripping again.

Perhaps Ralph Waldo Emerson described what I feel when I look at, not just trees but all of nature:

"The greatest wonder is that we can see these trees and not wonder more."

The wilderness fills me with a sense of wonder and awe, and to be a part of it, for even a short time, is a truly magical experience for me.

As I sit here and write this, my college days are drawing to a close. I have only one short month left before I graduate. And I know what I want to do. I will be spending the summer of 2010 working on the Northern Forest Canoe Trail. The organization has given me a summer job, and allowed me to return to the Trail I love, the Trail that gave me so much, and to give a little in return. To revisit those lakes, rivers, streams and portages, and to help to ensure that they can continue to be enjoyed, as I enjoyed them, for generations to come, is a gift that I shall treasure always. For this Trail, all other Trails, and all other rivers are still calling my name. It remains for me to decide where to go next, which call to answer. Then I will return to the place I love: the wilderness.

References Cited:

Beck, H. C. (1961). Forgotten Towns of Southern New Jersey. New Brunswick, New Jersey, Rutgers University Press.

Brakeley, J. T. (2010). Notes and Research of Patricia E. Brakeley. P. E. Brakeley.

Cohen, L., S. Cohen, et al. (2003). Old Forge: Gateway to the Adirondacks. Charleston, South Carolina, Arcadia Publishing.

Conover, G. (1991). Beyond the Paddle. Gardiner, Maine, Tilbury House.

De Sormo, M. C. (1975). Noah John Rondeau: Adirondack Hermit. Saranac Lake, New York, Adirondack Yesteryears, Inc.

Donaldson, A. L. (2001). A History of the Adirondacks. Fleischmanns, New York, Purple Mountain Press.

Donaldson, A. L. (2002). A History of the Adirondacks. Fleischmanns, New York, Purple Mountain Press.

Friedman, S. T. and K. Marden (2007). Captured! The Betty and Barney Hill UFO Experience. Franklin Lakes, New Jersey, New Page Books.

Goodson, L. (1999). There Was a Land, Flagstaff Memorial Chapel Association.

Harper, K. (2000). Give Me My Father's Body. South Royalton, Vermont, Steerforth Press.

Headley, J. T. (1853). The Second War With England. New York, New York, Charles Scribner.

Hochschild, H. K. (1962). Adirondack Steamboats on Raquette and Blue Mountain Lakes. Blue Mountain Lake, New York, Adirondack Museum.

Jamieson, P. (1981). Adirondack Canoe Waters. Glen Falls, New York, The Adirondack Mountain Club, Inc.

Jerome, C. (1994). An Adirondack Passage. New York, New York, HarperCollins Publishers, Inc.

Kaiser, H. H. (1986). Great Camps of the Adirondacks. Boston, Massachusetts, David R. Godine.

Kinchen, O. A. (1970). Confederate Operations in Canada and the North. North Quincy, Massachusetts, The Christopher Publishing House.

Koop, A. V. (1988). Stark Decency. Hanover, New Hampshire, University Press of New England.

Lonergan, C. V. (1974). The Northern Gateway: A History of Lake Champlain, Fort Mount Hope Society.

Murray, W. H. H. (1970). Adventures in the Wilderness. Syracuse, New York, Syracuse University Press.

New York State Archives (2010). "Camp Riverdale Records." Retrieved 5/7/2010, from http://iarchives.nysed.gov/xtf/view?docId=MS_70-12.xml.

Northern Forest Canoe Trail (2005). Map 2: Adirondack North Country (Central). Seattle, Washington, The Mountaineers Books.

Northern Forest Canoe Trail (2005). Map 4: Islands and Farms Region. Seattle, Washington, The Mountaineers Books.

Northern Forest Canoe Trail (2005). Map 5: Upper Missisquoi Valley. Seattle, Washington, The Mountaineers Books.

Northern Forest Canoe Trail (2005). Map 6: Northeast Kingdom. Seattle, Washington, The Mountaineers Books.

Northern Forest Canoe Trail (2005). Map 7: Great North Woods. Seattle, Washington, The Mountaineers Books.

Northern Forest Canoe Trail (2005). Map 8: Rangeley Lakes Region. Seattle, Washington, The Mountaineers Books.

Northern Forest Canoe Trail (2005). Map 9: Flagstaff Lake Region. Seattle, Washington, The Mountaineers Books.

Northern Forest Canoe Trail (2005). Map 11: Moosehead/Penobscot Region. Seattle, Washington, The Mountaineers Books.

Northern Forest Canoe Trail (2005). Map 12: Allagash Region - South. Seattle, Washington, The Mountaineers Books.

Northern Forest Canoe Trail (2005). Map 13: Allagash Region - North. Seattle, Washington, The Mountaineers Books.

Northern Forest Canoe Trail (2010). "NFCT Trail Overview." Retrieved 5/5/2010, from http://northernforestcanoetrail.org/AboutNFCT-2/NFCT-Trail-Overview-35.

Parker, E. L. (1996). Beyond Moosehead. Greenville, Maine, Moosehead Communications.

Poling Sr., J. (2000). The Canoe: An illustrated History. Woodstock, Vermont, The Countryman Press.

Randall, W. S. (1990). Benedict Arnold: Patriot and Traitor. New York, New York, William Morrow and Company.

Rich, L. D. (1942). We Took to the Woods. Philadelphia, Pennsylvania, J. B. Lippincott Company.

Rose, B. Z. (2007). John Stark: Maverick General. Waverley, Massachusetts, Treeline Press.

Ross, J. F. (2009). War on the Run. New York, New York, Bantam Books.

Sellers, C. C. (1930). Benedict Arnold: The Proud Warrior. New York, New York, Minton, Balch & Company.

Steele, T. S. (1882). Paddle and Portage. Boston, Massachusetts, Estes and Lauriat.

Stoddard, S. R. (1983). The Adirondacks Illustrated. Glen Falls, New York, Finch, Pruyn & Company , Inc.

The Ethan Allen Homestead Museum (2010). "Who Was Ethan Allen?". Retrieved 5/6/2010, from http://www.ethanallenhomestead.org/a-short-biography-of-ethan-allen.html.

Thoreau, H. D. (1950). The Maine Woods. New York, New York, Bramhall House.

Welsh, P. C. (1995). Jacks, Jobbers, and Kings: Logging in the Adirondacks, 1850-1950. Utica, New York, North Country Books, Inc.

www.HistoricVermont.org (2010). Vermont History Timeline.

Made in the USA
San Bernardino, CA
23 December 2013